THE
PART-TIME
REAL ESTATE
INVESTOR

How to Generate Huge Profits
While Keeping Your Day Job

REVISED 2ND EDITION

BY

Dan W. Blacharski

REVISED BY

Jim Kim

THE PART-TIME REAL ESTATE INVESTOR: HOW TO GENERATE HUGE PROFITS WHILE KEEPING YOUR DAY JOB

Copyright © 2016 Atlantic Publishing Group, Inc.

1405 SW 6th Avenue • Ocala, Florida 34471 • Phone 800-814-1132 • Fax 352-622-1875
Website: www.atlantic-pub.com • Email: sales@atlantic-pub.com
SAN Number: 268-1250

Library of Congress Cataloging-in-Publication Data

Names: Blacharski, Dan, 1959– author.
Title: The part-time real estate investor : how to generate huge profits while keeping your day job / by Dan W. Blacharski.
Description: 2 Edition. | Ocala : Atlantic Publishing Group, Inc., [2016] | Revised edition of the author's The part-time real estate investor, c2007. | Includes bibliographical references and index.
Identifiers: LCCN 2016043611 (print) | LCCN 2016048982 (ebook) | ISBN 9781601389466 (alk. paper) | ISBN 1601389469 (alk. paper) | ISBN 9781601389596 ()
Subjects: LCSH: Real estate investment—United States. | Real property—Purchasing—United States. | House buying—United States.
Classification: LCC HD255 .B53 2016 (print) | LCC HD255 (ebook) | DDC 332.63/240973—dc23
LC record available at https://lccn.loc.gov/2016043611

Printed in the United States

PROJECT MANAGER AND EDITOR: Rebekah Sack • rsack@atlantic-pub.com
INTERIOR LAYOUT AND JACKET DESIGN: Nicole Sturk • nicolejonessturk@gmail.com
COVER DESIGN: Jackie Miller • millerjackiej@gmail.com

Reduce. Reuse.
RECYCLE.

A decade ago, Atlantic Publishing signed the Green Press Initiative. These guidelines promote environmentally friendly practices, such as using recycled stock and vegetable-based inks, avoiding waste, choosing energy-efficient resources, and promoting a no-pulping policy. We now use 100-percent recycled stock on all our books. The results: in one year, switching to post-consumer recycled stock saved 24 mature trees, 5,000 gallons of ~~~~~~~~~~~~~~ ent of the total energy used f~~~~~~~~~~~~~~~~~~~~~he equivalent ~~~~~~~~~~~~~~~~~~~~~~~~~~~~~~ven for a y~~~

Current Check-Outs summary for NGUYEN, T
Wed Dec 06 15:25:37 EST 2017

Discover your destiny with the mo

BARCODE: 3339000296~~~~
TITLE: Discover MINEOLA
DELIVERY STOP: MINEOLA
DUE DATE: Jan 06 2018
STATUS: unknown
DESENSITIZED:

Over the years, we have a~~~~~~~~~~~~~~~~~~~~~~~~~~~~~~~~~~. First there was Bear and a~~~~~~~~~~~~~~~~~~~~~~~~~~have Kira, another rescue. They ~~~~~~~~~~~~~~~~e not just into our lives, but into the lives o~~~~~~~~

We want you to know a porti~~~~~ e profits of this book will be donated in Bear, Ginger and Scout's memory to local animal shelters, parks, conservation organizations, and other individuals and nonprofit organizations in need of assistance.

— ***Douglas & Sherri Brown,***
President & Vice-President of Atlantic Publishing

Table of Contents

PART ONE

ANYONE CAN BE A MILLIONAIRE

CHAPTER 1

Why Real Estate?

I haven't had a real job in 25 years.

For quite some time, my office has been wherever I choose to sit down. Right now, that's my hometown of South Bend, Indiana, but I've also worked from the California coast, Krakow, and Bangkok.

When you choose to take your vocational destiny in your own hands and stop working for other people, whether it's in real estate or anything else, your friends become envious, thinking that your glorious career is romantic and exciting. There is some excitement, true—a little romance if you're lucky—but mostly, it's just a lot of work. When you stop working for other people, you will first make the mistake of thinking you can make your own hours. While this is true to some extent, in reality, you will start work earlier and finish later than you did when you used to punch that time clock.

You may have purchased some of those books that purport to tell you how to work an hour a day and get rich in real estate. That's a popular claim to make because it sells a lot of books, but unfortunately, it's not true. Within the pages of *Part-time Real Estate Investor*, you'll learn about what is true and what is not, what is possible, and what you cannot (or should not) do. There may well come a point when you will be working only a few hours a day and taking in millions, but that point is not today. It will take a lot of hard work to get there.

Still other books purport to give you the "real secrets" of wealth — those miraculous, hidden strategies known only to a few elite individuals to make millions in real estate overnight.

The real, multi-million-dollar secret of the real estate investor elite is: *There are no secrets.* The "hidden strategies" that are kept secret by a mysterious millionaire's club are nonexistent. Are there some mysterious words you can utter to make real estate sellers like putty in your hands? Magic formulas that will make bankers cower before you? No. However, there are pieces of information, strategies, and tactics that are not very well known, and this is the information that I will present to you in this book.

WHY IS IT A GOOD INVESTMENT?

There are a lot of ways to make money, but real estate is one that stands out above the crowd. Why? Because everybody needs somewhere to live. One of the best ways to succeed as an entrepreneur is to have something that everybody either wants or needs. Now to be perfectly honest, it's not precisely true that every single person in America wants someplace to live. When I lived in San Francisco's Haight-Ashbury district, I made the acquaintance of a gentleman who lived in Golden Gate Park, standing on the principle that he simply did not wish to be part of "the system." He made his home in the midst of some dense brush on the far end of the park where he had fashioned a shelter out of some discarded scrap metal and wood, and he seemed quite happy with himself.

But outside of a handful of people like my hippie friend, almost all of us want someplace to live. People spend between a third and a half of their monthly income to get it. If you're the one who provides it, you can become very rich indeed. Here's a few interesting statistics: in the United States, as of the second quarter of 2016, the U.S. Census Bureau reports that owner-occupied housing units accounted for 54.9 percent of total housing units, while renter-occupied units accounted for 32.4 percent. And according to RealtyTrac, the median sales price of single-family homes and condos as of early 2016 was $210,000. That's an 11 percent increase over the previous year. In fact, as of March, the value of such homes had risen for 49 months in row. The market has been hot indeed, exceeding or approaching record values in many areas. Nationally, the market hit a peak in July 2005, when the median sale price hit $228,000.

With more than half of homes in America being owner-occupied, and with the market for real estate so strong, it's clear that homeownership remains highly valued in our society, though plenty of people continue to rent. What's important for you as an investor to remember is that buying real estate is not out of reach. It's not just for the rich. It's not even just for the credit-worthy. Do you think that all Americans have good credit? Think again. Here's a little "secret" I'll let you in on: you can buy a home — or buy a dozen homes — with the worst credit rating in the world. In my own case, I purchased a historic, 12-room restored Victorian home last year for my wife and me to live in. But after two previous marriages that ended in disaster, my credit left a lot to be desired. In fact, if you were to run my credit report, the computer would gag and cough, probably say a few swear words, and then would spit out a report with big red letters stamped across the front, saying "Don't *Ever* Lend This Guy Money." Underpaid clerks at Experian probably spend their break time and laughing at my credit report. The salesperson at the car lot that advertises "we finance anybody" would jump out the back window of the showroom if I walked in the door. But even I can buy a house. Or a dozen houses. You can, too. You just have to know a few tricks of the trade, know where to look, and know what to ask of whom.

UNCLE SAM LOVES HOMEOWNERS

Ever since the Great Depression of the 1930s, Uncle Sam has taken a very large and active role in promoting homeownership in America. The government's social agenda is to make homeownership attractive and possible to a broad range of people in all income categories. The good news is that not only does Uncle Sam love homeowners, if you're in the business of real estate investing, you are turning more people into homeowners, and Uncle Sam will love you, too.

Before the creation of the Federal Housing Administration (FHA) in 1934, mortgages were usually short-term instruments. Borrowers needed to come up with a very large amount of money—as much as 50 percent—to put as a down payment, and they very likely would have had to re-qualify for the mortgage every few years. Lots of people lost their homes during the 1930s, and there were unscrupulous bankers who refused to re-qualify borrowers for any excuse, just to seize their property. Of course, there are still unscrupulous bankers today, and it's still possible for someone to lose a home, but the process has changed for the better. The concept of FHA is a simple one: Borrowers are able to purchase mortgage insurance from the FHA, which protects bankers in case of default. In addition, a secondary mortgage market was created with the establishment of "Fannie Mae" and "Freddie Mac," which actually purchase mortgages from banks, allowing the banks to make more loans than they would otherwise.

The point of this brief history lesson is this: The U.S. government has a social agenda of promoting homeownership. Most people agree that it's a good agenda. And as most people know, when the government decides it wants to accomplish something, enormous amounts of money get spent throughout every level of the economy. You want to be on the receiving end of some of this money. That's not to say the government is going to give it to you directly—although in some cases, it's as good as that. In chapter 24, we'll look at some of the preferential tax treatments you will receive as a homeowner and real estate investor. As an indirect result of this social agenda, it has become much easier over the past 80+ years to make big money in real estate—and even to get rich from nothing.

PHILOSOPHY OF REAL ESTATE INVESTING

If you put $10,000 in the bank, you may be able to receive five percent return, or about $500 a year. If you put it in the stock market and trade conservatively, you could reasonably expect to get ten percent, or $1,000 a year.

But $1,000 a year is "extra money." That's clearly not enough to live on. I don't know anybody who would turn down $1,000 if I handed it to them, but in reality, it doesn't go that far. What we want to do is to take that same $10,000, or whatever amount you may have, and balloon it into a fortune large enough for you to quit your day job and retire in a few years.

There are two ways to go about real estate investing. The mainstream method, which your bankers and investment counselors will tell you to do, would be to take that $10,000, take out a mortgage from a traditional lender, and buy a rental property. Let's say that you are able to purchase a small rental home for $100,000 in a working-class neighborhood in the Midwest. With 10 percent down, you will have a mortgage of $90,000, and if you have a mortgage that carries for example, 7 percent interest, your monthly payments would be about $600. Add on another $100 a month to cover taxes and insurance, and your total monthly expense base is $700. After looking at the market, you see that you can reasonably expect to rent the house out for about $800 a month, so you have a profit of $100 a month, or $1200 a year. That's 12 percent return on your investment. That's better than the stock market example above, but not that much better, and buying shares of an S&P500 fund is certainly easier than maintaining a rental house. If you only get 12 percent a year from your rental house, you're better off with a more passive investment. With this example, your stock market fund will pay you $200 a year less, but you'll have a lot more free time to pursue other deals.

But instead of trying to take a certain amount of money and earn a percentage return every year, the better philosophy of real estate investing is to look at that money as a grubstake—start-up money. You don't just want to get a 10 percent return. You're starting a business. And you want that business to bring you enough money to live comfortably. And yes, you can do that with $10,000. As a matter of fact, you can do it with no money at all. That business may well involve maintaining some rental properties, but in this book, we'll talk more about buying and selling and the greater profits that can be realized.

FOREIGN MARKETS

Although the focus of this book is making money on real estate in the U.S., you don't have to limit yourself to one country. Fortunes are ready to be made in emerging countries all around the world. India's emerging middle class and growing economy are creating a tremendous need for quality homes, for example. There are some laws you don't have to worry about in the U.S., however. For example, in India and many other countries, foreigners are not allowed to have 100 percent ownership of businesses or property. This means you may have to take a local partner. In fact, many Westerners are growing rich today through successful partnerships in India, China, and other countries. An indirect way of making foreign investments is through investment funds in which you take a passive role and let the fund managers deal with all of the legalities and send you a check every month.

Although there are some risks, and you have to understand the laws, culture, and some of the language, there is a big upside—potential growth in an emerging market that simply does not exist in a mature market. My wife, a native of Thailand, owns a substantial amount of very valuable property there because her very wise mother bought it long ago when land was cheap and Thailand was still a developing country. The lesson here is to not limit yourself to your own hometown. It's a great place to start, but you don't have to stop there. The truly successful entrepreneur knows no boundaries.

LET'S START MAKING MONEY!

Whether you're already an investor or just have a little money you want to put to work for you, or have nothing at all, this book is for you. There are dozens of conventional, and some not-so-conventional ways to buy property, and it's possible for virtually anybody, in any situation, to get into real estate as an investment opportunity. And yes, you *can* get rich.

CHAPTER 2

Finding Your Strategy

There are specific techniques to use, strategies and tactics to study, and business plans to be created. There is work to be done, and you may even have to get your hands dirty doing a little renovation from time to time, but the most important effort involves your head, not your hands.

Achieving success in real estate, or any other field for that matter, requires a certain state of mind. First is the cultivation of an attitude. Many people won't succeed or won't even try, because they feel that a certain level of success is simply beyond them or reserved only for an elite group of "connected" people. Realizing that wealthy people are just like you will help you to overcome that level of intimidation and become one of them.

SOME STATISTICS

Chances are you know people who are fabulously wealthy, but you don't even realize it.

A person who "has it made" isn't always the cigar-chomping, limousine-riding, flashy wheeler-dealer of movies and cartoons. He or she may be your neighbor who drives a late-model but second-hand car, has a good percent of his wealth in his home and retirement account, and goes to work every day. He probably has some side deals going on, however, in addition to his day job. He probably has some real estate holdings, some stocks and bonds, or some sort of small business he runs part-time. He probably didn't go to Harvard. More likely, he went to the local community college or state university. He may not have inherited wealth; odds are he built his wealth up from nothing.

There are well over two million millionaires in the United States alone, and that's an encouraging statistic. Given that the population of the United States is about 325 million, that means that more than one in 150 people is a millionaire! If you stand on the corner of a busy downtown and see about 150 people walk by, one is a millionaire. Let's say there were 450 people in your high school graduating class. Three of your classmates are millionaires by now.

IS WEALTH ONLY FOR OTHER PEOPLE?

Here's an example of the idea that wealth and opportunity are only for the privileged:

I am married to an immigrant, a lovely woman from Thailand. For a while, we ran our own import shop. One day, a friend was talking about opening up a store and said the prospect seemed out of reach for her. She was a bit envious of us and wondered how we did it. She thought she had all the answers, and told me that she believed most small shops were owned by immigrants, because of some mysterious government program she heard of that gives money to new immigrants to start their own businesses. And what's more, she told me that they don't have to pay any taxes!

I was amazed by her negative attitude. Of course, there is no such program, and there are obviously no special tax breaks for immigrants who own their own shops. Shop owners for the most part get no special breaks, immigrant or not. Yet it's true, a lot of small shops are owned by immigrants. And more power to them. Why? Because we who grew up here tend to be a bit more complacent. We tend to think about running a business as an enormous task with insurmountable obstacles, something that takes huge amounts of money up-front, and something you must be well-connected to implement. Opening up a store is "for other people," we say. And so we don't do it.

In the case of my friend, she believed "other people" were privileged immigrants. Others believe that "other people" are those who are well connected, went to Ivy League schools, or have inherited wealth. Somebody that is new to this country hasn't encountered that same mental roadblock and comes here to experience the American dream, thinking that it still exists while many Americans have already given up on it.

Remarkably, they achieve it. Why? Because they haven't grown up being told that they can't, so they're not afraid to jump right in and do something, while we here grew up being told that we can't. I know I grew up that way. I was expected to get a "good job" in the factory and stick with it. We here tend to think there are too many obstacles to getting wealthy. It's more of a state of mind than a state of wealth.

THE MYTH OF SECURITY

All of our lives, our parents, our teachers, and our jobs reinforce the message that security is important, and so we take the offer from a larger company rather than the entrepreneurial one. We put money in certain banks because their commercials tell us that our money is secure there. We depend on our pensions, thinking that they too are secure. If we invest in the stock market, we buy blue chip stocks instead of small cap stocks, thinking they are secure. We get married, thinking that our relationships are secure, and we select certain neighborhoods to live in, thinking that our homes will be secure.

Before you become wealthy, you must blast through the security myth and realize that there is, in fact, no such thing. Believing in security is not conducive to getting rich. It is conducive to "getting by." Striving for security above all else allows you to rise to a more-or-less comfortable level and stay there. It does not allow you to get rich. That's because if you are preoccupied with being secure, you do not take risks, you do not try new things, and you do not go into business for yourself. If you do buy real estate while you are preoccupied with security, you will buy only using traditional methods your banker tells you to use, and you will buy properties that deliver a reasonable but not superior return. You most certainly will not get rich.

When I lived in Bangkok, I studied Buddhist philosophy and enjoyed the company and guidance of Buddhist monks who offered an enlightening viewpoint on living. Getting rich is really not something a Buddhist monk would have an interest in. But this Eastern philosophy does have many practical applications for the world, even for the wealthy.

The one thing I was taught that sticks out in my mind is *"the impermanence of all things."*

I considered that phrase time and time again. After hearing the monks talk about it, I thought about my own hometown. In the 1960s, the Studebaker plant was a major employer there. Most of the local economy depended on it, and everybody in town believed that there would always be a Studebaker. The carmaker gave our town prosperity and the *illusion* of security. But they stopped making Studebakers in 1965, and not only did thousands of people lose good-paying jobs that they relied on, but they also lost their pensions. People who had worked for 20 years or more for one company spent their entire working lives believing that they had job security and a pension that was absolutely rock-solid. They were wrong.

Freeing yourself from the illusion of security is the first step to becoming truly wealthy. Being rid of the notion of security frees you from being unduly tied to a single concept, doing things the way they have always been done. If you are free from that stubborn adherence to all things secure, you will be free to try new things, to experiment, to negotiate. Wealth involves risk. You will be free to innovate and think of new ways to get rich. Some of them won't work. Some will. Don't be afraid to try.

THINK LIKE A PERSON OF WEALTH

The first thing you need to do before embarking on your real estate investor career is to make a list of all the obstacles you see in your way. You may be able to add to this list:

1. I have bad credit.

2. I have no investment capital.

3. I have no higher education.

4. I don't have connections.

5. I have too many debts to pay off.

Study your list carefully.

Then destroy it. Because those obstacles are all completely irrelevant.

Of course, most objections get down to one thing—fear of change or risk. We tend to be afraid of losing it all, even if we don't have that much to lose. We become paralyzed by that fear and spend our lives seeking out some little secure corner of the world to occupy. We get jobs at the post office. We put back the flashy necktie and put on the plain blue one. We stay in bad marriages. We put off that trip around the world we have always wanted to take. We stick with what we have, even if what we have is inadequate, just because it is familiar. We manage with our limited income, and we stay comfortable in our mediocre jobs to avoid being afraid. In the end, we regret not being more adventurous.

FAILURE IS NOT A BAD THING

Just as there is no such thing as security, so too there is no such thing as failure. We may set out to accomplish something but end up accomplishing something else, but that is not failure. It is merely the accomplishment of another goal that we hadn't originally considered. What we accomplish may be learning a lesson, or gaining a new insight. One business idea may crash and burn, but maybe it will leave us with another great idea that will make millions.

I've met several people who berated themselves for failure. Some even believed mistakenly that if they failed to achieve a certain level of prosperity or accomplish a certain goal, that they are not only failures, they are *bad people*.

There are even some spiritual beliefs that center on prosperity, promoting the concept that success comes only to those who have faith in a certain concept or say a certain set of words to one or another deity or prophet. So then failure means you did not have enough faith and you are not good enough to merit what you sought. Say your prayers, by all means, but don't wait for God to give you a million dollars. You have to put in some effort of your own.

Take note: After you finish reading this book and start making real estate deals, it is possible that you may not complete your first deal. It may go wrong, you may not accomplish what you set out to accomplish, the other guy may be a crook who steals your money, or you may just not make as much profit as you anticipated. *This does not mean you are a bad person.* It doesn't mean you lacked any sort of faith, uttered the wrong prayers, or are somehow unworthy, or that the Universe, God, or the Law of Karma has it out for you. Just take a look at the deal, take a lesson from it, and do it again. Maybe you didn't make money from the deal, but you will learn something, and knowledge is power.

The most wealthy and successful entrepreneurs are, in fact, monumental failures.

Sure, they may be multi-millionaires today, but in most cases, they got there by failing, looking at those failures, and then trying again. They got to be rich by learning from their mistakes, and by just simply continuing to try new things. Getting rich is to some degree a game of strategy and intellect, and to some degree, it's just a matter of staying in the game. Wealth accumulation can be a numbers game. It's not likely that you'll make money on every deal, but you'll make money in most of them. If you try one time only, you have a pretty good shot at not making any money. If you try 10 times, you'll win some of the time, and you will start accumulating some wealth.

There is nothing magic about becoming wealthy. It *can* happen to you so that you can quit your day job.

CHAPTER 3

Real Estate as a Business

You can get started part-time while keeping your day job. Buying and selling real estate isn't just a rich man's game. You don't even need a lot of money or even good credit to become involved in this lucrative business.

But it is just that: a *business*. The only way to succeed is to treat it as one. As we saw in Chapter 2, yes, making a bundle in real estate does take a certain mindset, a philosophy of success, and the ability to "think like a rich person." But that doesn't mean playing golf and buying a new Mercedes. It means having a strategy.

The images of a rich lifestyle are only the outcome. Focusing on the *results* of wealth won't get you rich; focusing on the *strategy* of wealth will.

LOOKING THE PART

The first thing to do before you even negotiate your first deal is to realize that you are starting a business. When you start a business, there are certain trappings that are necessary. That is to say, if you look like a businessperson and act like a businessperson, you will be treated like one. That's why the little things like printed business cards and good clothes are important. Creating an atmosphere of professionalism and confidence around you opens doors.

Suppose, for example, you are a homeowner in trouble and are looking for someone to bail you out. Suppose two guys approach you, offering to make your back payments and a little extra, give you plenty of time to move out, and save you from foreclosure. The first guy to come to your door with this offer is wearing droopy pants that come up only to his knees, a sideways baseball cap, and a sports jersey. He writes down his phone number on the back of an old phone bill receipt. The second guy drives up in a clean second-hand car, is wearing a business suit, and has printed business cards. Maybe the first guy has more money, but chances are, you'll make your deal with the second one because of the first impression.

In Chapter 2, I talked about overcoming your intimidation and fear of rich people, by realizing that they are just like us. But one thing you'll notice is that people who have money have a certain image, and that image sometimes cultivates the feeling of separation between "us" and "them." If you're a homeowner in foreclosure, you don't want someone just like you to bail you out, you want one of "them," because you think "they" are the ones with the money. When you look like "them," people will treat you like "them." You have to walk a fine line between creating sympathy and establishing a rapport, but at the same time set yourself up as someone who has special expertise and something unique to offer.

It's remarkable what a good suit can do. Having lived in San Francisco's Haight-Ashbury district, I have a few unusual stories to tell. Of course, I had the requisite long hair, beard, and earring at the time, and I dressed according to the style of the region, like a hippie. When I saw my fellow hippies on the street, they greeted me and called me "brother." We would sit in a coffeehouse and read poetry at each other.

When I got a job downtown in the financial district, I started wearing a suit and tie every day, and I tied my long hair back in a neat ponytail, which in San Francisco's financial district is still considered "business chic." But then, everything changed. Instead of "brother," I became "mister," and people asked me for money. I got better tables at restaurants. People respected me at my new job. I was still the same person, but I had more credibility because of my new appearance.

Sometimes, a clean suit may be the only thing you have going for you, so you make the most of what you have. A good friend of mine was known as a "white knight." Instead of buying foreclosed homes, he bought corporations that were on the verge of failure and turned them around. But in reality, he started out as a working-class guy, had no money, and was in fact bankrupt. But, as they say, he "cleaned up real nice," and had loads of self-confidence. One day, he rode up to a certain office in a rented limousine, and walked into a corporate boardroom in his clean suit. He told them what they wanted to hear, laid out a very detailed strategy for saving the day, and walked away with the keys to the kingdom. He didn't lay a single dollar on the table. He became a "white knight" because he looked and acted like one. Nobody ever knew he was broke. Of course, he went on to make millions.

$$$ *Part-Time Real Estate Investor Tip* $$$

Before you buy a single piece of real estate, start your real estate business with the following:

- Printed business cards with your phone numbers and email address

- An attractive (but not too flashy) website with details of services you can offer

- Business attire

- A clean and well-maintained car (even if it's used)

- A briefcase full of printed forms, ready to go, such as lease agreements and purchase documents.

SET UP A HOME OFFICE

There's a lot to be said about the advantages of a home office, and being able to work in your bathrobe, but sometimes it's not as easy as it sounds.

First of all, it's essential that you have a home office, even if it's just a small desk in the corner of your living room. Create some separate space that is dedicated just to your real estate business. This will do two things for you: It will help you stay organized, and it will help you stay focused because you will have a central location for your business-related materials, instead of trying to remember where you left those land contracts—in your sock drawer or in the kids' toy box? Different parts of your home have different meanings and associations. Have you ever tried to do work while sitting on the couch where you usually watch television? Or on your bed? It usually doesn't turn out well.

Of course, as a real estate expert, you must know that maintaining a home office gives you a good tax break, too.

It goes without saying that you'll be spending a lot of time on the internet via your computer and probably your smartphone as well. There are plenty of online resources available to you, often at no cost, so it would be wise to invest to make sure your internet connection is up to speed.

GOALS AND MILESTONES

"I will have $_____ by the time I'm _____ years old."

And we should all have a goal. Pick a goal for your earning and an age that is older than you are, insert them into the above phrase, and write it on your message board. These are the goals in life that keep us on task and doing what we must.

There are a lot of small steps along the way, and you need to set those out in writing as well. I have a friend who comes over to visit often, and the first thing he does is walk into my home office and look at my chalkboard. That's because I have a goal, and I write it up there every week. My goal is to make a certain amount of money every single week. Every day, I write on the board what I've earned, and at the end of the week I total it up, and most times, I make that goal. Sure, you can have a goal of earning $100,000 this year, but the end of the year is a long way off. Break those larger goals down into smaller ones. It makes it more achievable, and you can stay in touch with how you are progressing more easily.

NO MAN IS AN ISLAND – HOW TO GET OTHERS TO HELP YOU

You will be surprised at the number of people who will be willing to help you. The vast majority of these people will offer help in the way of advice, and for the most part, you should ignore them. The world is full of arm-chair experts and well-meaning busybodies, but if somebody hasn't achieved a superior level of success themselves, their advice is usually not worth much. People will tell you that your strategies are too risky, that you shouldn't do this or that, and that you should only use tried and true, mainstream, conventional, and conservative methods for buying real estate. These people will be real estate agents and bankers, the two categories of people to ignore the most. If you take one thing from this book, remember this: *The filthy rich don't get to be filthy rich by being conservative.*

Someone who owns properties and is making money in real estate may be worth listening to. Surprisingly, people who have made a fortune love to talk about how they did it. It's a common trait among the rich. You would think that they would want to keep their secrets to themselves, and in fact, there are a lot of books and newsletters out there trying to get your money by saying that they will reveal their secrets to you for a fee. In fact, the rich don't like to keep secrets. Most of the ones I've met have enjoyed their success to such a degree that they're as eager as a teenager the day after prom night to tell their stories.

BECOME A REAL ESTATE EXPERT

A wise man (or maybe it was a wise guy,) once told me the definition of "expert," informing me that the word must be broken into its two parts: An "ex" is a has-been, and a "spurt" is a little drip.

The guys with the real estate licenses, the MBAs, and the fancy titles that banks hand out don't really have that much up on you. In fact, you will have something up on them, because these conventional players have boxed themselves into a set way of doing things. You're not going to do that, and in the end, you will make more money than they will.

Courses in real estate may have some value, but they are not necessary, unless you want to get a real estate license. You can give yourself a good education. Real estate investing is a "learn as you go" process.

Gather as much knowledge about real estate, paperwork, processes, and your local markets as you can. Talk to other investors, and learn as much as you can about renovation. In Chapter 25, we'll talk more about fixing up homes and will again revisit the illusion of the expert. You can educate yourself about home repair and avoid a lot of unnecessary contractor bills.

Read the classified section of the paper every day to get a feel for the market and the prices of homes. Drive around different neighborhoods and try to spot opportunities, just for practice, before you make your first buy. Education is a continuing process, but if you think like an expert, you will become one very quickly.

CHAPTER 4

Get Rich Quick

There are a lot of real estate books, seminars, and programs out there. Some are useful, some are a waste of money, and some are downright illegal.

THE "GET RICH QUICK" MENTALITY

When you pay your money and attend a real estate seminar, you'll notice one thing: The leader of the seminar has more energy than a room full of preschoolers in a candy factory. He's literally bouncing off the walls as he gives his presentation, and his energy is engaging and exciting. If he hasn't gotten rich in real estate already, he's certainly getting rich holding seminars and writing books. I don't have that energy level and won't be holding any seminars. You'll see the same energy level at multi-level marketing seminars, where you walk away convinced that it's a good idea to try to get people to buy a bottle of some exotic tropical fruit juice that is said to cure all of mankind's ills for $40 a pop.

As a side note on the latter, I lived in a tropical country where those exotic fruits grow, and I used to buy the juices for the equivalent of about 50 cents a bottle. They're quite tasty, probably very healthy, and there are local anecdotes about their medicinal qualities. But it's not going to cure all the diseases they say it will, and it's definitely not worth $40 a bottle. That's why I like real estate as an investment opportunity. Many of the multi-layered marketing (MLM) deals have overblown claims and attempt to sell goods that are overpriced. Real estate isn't like that.

Also be wary of the outrageous claims that are made by real estate seminar promoters. Outrageous claims are part and parcel of the sales business. A promoter may have made millions of dollars' worth of transactions, he says, but is he offering any proof? Is he showing you his last year's 1040? Does he still have a day job at the 7/11? Probably not a good sign. You have to ask, why is this guy who has made millions going around holding seminars instead of making more real estate deals himself? You'll probably get some sort of line about "wanting to share my wisdom," or "wanting to bring opportunities to deserving people." That is rubbish. People who hold money-making seminars are not altruistic. If you believe they are, ask them if they will put off their seminar fee until after you make your first million and see what they say. They hold seminars to make money, plain and simple. Is the seminar even worth the money they're asking?

DUE DILIGENCE

If you are being asked to subscribe to a program, newsletter, seminar, series of tapes, or some other sort of real estate education program, take time to consider before you jump into it. If the cost is significant (for example, more than the cost of this book), take time to plan what you really want to get out of it. As we've said before, there really are no secrets in real estate wealth building. But a seminar may well be worth a few hundred dollars if it's something that will tell you about the things you don't know.

WHAT'S POSSIBLE

We talk about what's possible, and specifically how to accomplish what's possible, in Part Two. You've heard about some of these things and have wondered if it can really be done. Yes, they can. To satisfy your curiosity, here's a short list:

- It is possible to buy a house with bad credit.

- It is possible to buy a house with no money down.

- It is possible to buy a house without involving a conventional bank or mortgage lender.

- It is possible to make big money buying fixer-uppers.

- You can "flip" properties, sometimes even buying them and selling them at the same time, for profit.

- You can profit by investing in houses in blighted areas. (And no, you don't have to be a slumlord.)

WHAT'S NOT POSSIBLE

You may run across local ordinances and laws that thwart your get-rich-quick scheme. For example, you may decide to buy an old house and convert it into apartments, or you may decide to rent out individual rooms in the house to college students. (In places where this is allowed, you can get a lot more rental income out of your property than you could by just renting it out as a single-family dwelling.) But, before you go down that path, check out the local laws; the neighborhoods may not be zoned for these uses.

Some of the shadier real estate gurus engage in and promote activities that amount to mortgage fraud that could land you in jail. Schemes that artificially inflate the price of a property above market and then use that artificially inflated price to obtain a mortgage for more than the house is worth are illegal. Such schemes are carried out and form the basis of some of the "no-money-down" deals that real estate gurus claim can be done. But bankers like to go by their own set of rules, and when people skirt those rules, bankers have the force of law behind them. If no bank is involved, playing with the price of a home is no crime. Many laws today are written for (and sometimes by) bankers, and they're not afraid to use them. There are a million ways a real estate investor can defraud a bank in a real estate deal. Don't use them. There are other legitimate ways to do business — the banks still might not like them, but there's nothing they can do so long as there's no mortgage fraud involved.

Here's a prime example of how the laws are written for bankers. Mortgage fraud is only fraud when it involves a mortgage lender or bank. If you claim that a house worth $200,000 is really worth $220,000 and try to get a mortgage from a bank based on that $220,000 value, you have committed a crime. But, if you have a house that has a market value of $200,000, but then sell it directly (on land contract, or "subject to" contract) to a buyer for $220,000 and cut the bank out of the action, no crime has been committed.

WHAT'S NOT VERY LIKELY

There are some schemes that are bandied about by real estate promoters that sometimes work, but more often than not, they are a waste of time. Once in a while it works, and then it gets a lot of press. Even though such schemes don't usually work, they are still good to know, because there will be that one time when it will work and you will make money.

Here's one example: You find someone in foreclosure and offer to "take the house off their hands." It is then offered as a no-money-down scheme that usually won't work. The offer is that you will pay any arrearage due and take over payments subject to the underlying lien, allowing the homeowner to walk away. Some promoters even claim to be able to convince the homeowners to pay them money directly. Do you think somebody is actually going to pay you money to take their house away from them? *Not very likely.* When it works, which is not often, this is wonderful, and we'll talk more about this technique in Part Two. But in most cases, the homeowners don't just want to walk away, and they certainly don't want to pay you for the privilege of doing so. They may want some money out of the deal. In most cases, they are in financial trouble and may not even have money to move out. Also, this scheme is highly dependent on finding a homeowner who is willing to trust you to make the payments, because you're not really formally assuming the loan from the bank, you're just making the payments on behalf of the distressed homeowner in exchange for their claim on the property. The homeowner's name will still be on the note. Obviously, a homeowner would be very reluctant to take part in such a scheme.

$$$ *Part-Time Real Estate Investor Tip* $$$

I have known real estate investors who have gotten very excited about making money once they've figured out some of the techniques they can use, and they figure that they should work as quickly as possible and accumulate as much real estate as they possibly can in the shortest period of time. In many such cases, real estate empires built so quickly are like houses of cards that can come crashing down with the slightest breeze.

REAL ESTATE MYTHS

There are still a few legends floating around about spectacular deals that frankly are just not possible. Lots of people waste time and money trying to follow these mythical strategies, so let's dispel some of them right now.

Myth #1: The biggest example of this is the "outrageous bargain" myth. You cannot buy a HUD home, bank-owned property, or foreclosure for "pennies on the dollar." There are, to be sure, exceptionally good bargains out there, but don't believe it when people tell you that a bank will sell a foreclosure for the balance due "just to get it off their books."

Myth #2: You should always use a real estate agent for any transaction, a myth perpetrated obviously by real estate agents. In fact, agents are useful for individual homebuyers who just want to buy a single property to live in, but if you're going pro and trying to make money as an investor, you'll want to avoid their fees as often as possible—or better yet, get a license yourself.

Myth #3: You need to have a lot of money. Absolutely not true. This is another myth perpetrated by bankers. You can get started in real estate with next to nothing or even with nothing at all.

Myth #4: Buy and hold is always a good strategy because real estate always increases in value. As I follow-up below, there are such things as real estate bubbles, and it is very possible for real estate to lose out in value over time if you make the wrong decision on location.

Myth #5: Make sure your investment property is in perfect condition, and require the seller to correct any and all problems before the deal. In short, this is a very limiting strategy. In fact, your best bargains and your greatest profits will be made on the ugly, flawed homes that nobody else wants.

IS THERE A REAL ESTATE BUBBLE?

There are many stories circulating about people who purchased a home (often in California) and then sold it for double the price a few years later. Many of these stories are true, and that's why I no longer live in California.

There continue to be regional real estate bubbles in the United States, but there is not a general, countrywide bubble. I would not, for example, invest in real estate in San Francisco, San Diego, Palo Alto, or anywhere else where a 900-square-foot crackerbox home costs more than a million dollars. That's unsustainable in the long term, and yes, in those places, there may well be a bubble. And all bubbles eventually *will* pop.

For the greatest opportunity and the best stability, make your investments in places where a working man can still buy a home. Sure, it is possible that your million-dollar two-bedroom ranch home with a postage stamp sized yard will increase $100,000 in value by next year, but it's just as likely that it will decrease by that much. Areas like Silicon Valley and San Francisco that have seen unrealistic spiraling real estate costs over the past decade or so have pushed out the middle class that forms the real backbone of American homeownership. When a large city loses its middle class, there will eventually be a crash in its housing market.

As a real estate investor, you will almost always make more money by selling ordinary homes to ordinary middle class working people than you will by selling million-dollar homes to wealthy people. Given a choice between buying a million-dollar property in sunny California or 10 properties for $100,000 each in Mishawaka, Indiana, I'll go with Mishawaka. Bubbles must eventually burst. There is no housing bubble in the heartland.

CHAPTER 5

The Markets

Real estate investing depends to a large degree on location, but the greatest profits aren't always where you think they will be. "Hot," rapidly growing real estate markets aren't always the best place for investors. If you're already a multi-millionaire, these hot markets will present you with some good opportunities, and if you're in that boat, you probably don't need this book. For most of us who want to make our first million or even half million from nothing, the place to start is much different.

HIGH-VALUE DEALS AND WHY THEY'RE NOT ALWAYS A GOOD IDEA

If you're going into the business of buying and selling real estate, you're trafficking in a lot more than bricks and mortar. You're selling the American Dream. Everybody wants it.

The U.S. real estate market, as of mid-2016, strikes many experts as remarkably healthy. In July 2016, new homes were bought at an annual rate of 654,000, according to the U.S. Census Bureau. That's the highest since October 2007, before the so-called Great Recession of 2008-2009. Many communities have fully recovered from the housing market crash of 2008. In some cases, real estate values are soaring past all-time highs. The median value of a home in the U.S. hit $310,000 in June 2016, up from $185,000 in 2004.

Sensing a strong market for first-time homebuyers, notably millennial buyers, homebuilders are stepping up their activity. They have initiated work to erect new homes at a very rapid pace — about one million per month — in early 2016. That's up from 478,000 per month back in mid- to early 2015.

It's fair to say that the American Dream is alive and well.

Why is this important? For two reasons; first, it provides evidence that real estate is a good place to put your money, whether you own a single home or 100. Second, understanding these averages gives you a good idea of where the real estate market's "sweet spot" is.

The sweet spot is that area where homes will sell relatively quickly and provide you with a good profit, without requiring much up-front capital. Homes that are priced at the median value or under are affordable to more people, and if you deal in homes that do not exceed this price, you will be able to make more deals and turn them over faster. Everybody has heard stories about the California investors who buy and sell million dollar homes, but how many deals a year do you think they make? How long do they have to sit on a million-dollar home before finding a buyer? Unless you are incredibly wealthy, dealing in these high-value homes puts too much risk on a single deal. Sometimes, individual deals don't go the way you think they will. Any given home may sit on the market longer than you think, and the longer your money is tied up in any one deal, the greater your opportunity cost is. You may reap a big profit at the end of a million-dollar real estate deal, but take into account the opportunity cost and the risk factor. You need money to be able to support that million-dollar home if it sits on the market for six months. It happens more often than people want to admit: a big real estate deal going bad because the investor cannot sustain the loans until it sells.

Let's take a look at another deal. Suppose you find a property you want to buy for a million dollars, and you're pretty confident you can flip it for $1.1 million in short order. That's a cool $100,000 profit. But unless you have a million in cash, you're probably taking on some loans, and a 30-year mortgage for a million bucks, along with taxes and insurance, will run you about $8,000 a month. Now, suppose the market softens, and the house sits on the market for six months; and it sells for $1,050,000 instead of $1,100,000. You've paid on the loans for six months, so you've put about $48,000 into it already. As you can see, almost all your profit has evaporated.

That's why the big deals are risky and not always profitable. Many of the real estate investment seminars will tell you that it's possible for a small-time investor with very little capital to make multimillion-dollar real estate deals, and that is indeed true. If you're very lucky, you can make such a deal, and the property will sell for a profit the next day. But if it doesn't, you may be on a very short road to bankruptcy.

$$$ *Part-Time Real Estate Investor Tip* $$$

I've always gone by what I call the "circus juggler" philosophy of wealth building: Always have a half dozen balls in the air at any given time. That way, you probably have at least one performing project, a couple in the works, and one or two that just aren't going to cut it. As time goes on, drop the ones that don't work, add a couple more, and move on. Using this philosophy, a real estate investor won't put all available resources into a single deal, because if you drop that one, you have nothing left. And make no mistake, some deals will break. But if you have five more deals cooking at the same time, your loss won't be as devastating.

You may be able to buy into a property with very little or no money down, but that's only the starting point. If you're buying that property with no money down, you're 100 percent leveraged, and that works only if you're guaranteed an almost immediate turnover. But there are no guarantees in life, even in the real estate business. You may still need enough capital to sustain the loans while it sells. If you're talking about a $100,000 fixer-upper, you may be able to sustain that out of your own back pocket for a few months; but for a multimillion-dollar property, it's out of the question for most of us. The quick lesson here is not to get too excited about the prospect of high-value, no-money-down deals.

BREAD AND BUTTER PROPERTIES

The greatest profits percentage-wise, and the safest investments, aren't in those multi-million dollar deals or in luxury movie-star properties in Beverly Hills. Your bread and butter investments, the properties that will earn you steady income and allow you to build wealth over time, are the ones that are below the median price—the homes that ordinary people can buy.

Keep in mind: there's no law that says you have to invest in your own hometown. If you live in San Francisco, and you are a homeowner, your home is worth an average of about $1.13 million as of 2016, and there is little chance for creative back-door financing. But, you can make plenty of deals in smaller cities in the heartland, where the median price of a home is far lower.

THE BEST AND WORST CITIES FOR REAL ESTATE INVESTMENT

Real estate agents will tell you that "location, location, and location" are the three most important things in real estate, but what they want to sell and what you as an investor want to buy are two completely different things. Real estate agents sell properties to people who want to live in them, and it's in their best interest, since they work on commission, to promote the most expensive properties possible. Real estate agents make big money selling incredibly overpriced mansions, but for the most part, real estate speculators do not.

Let's revisit San Francisco for a moment. Homeowners in that majestic city have been blessed by an extremely strong market. Many of them purchased their homes years ago, when they were much more affordable. But this surge in the real estate market has unfortunately priced many residents out of the market. They simply can no longer afford to buy real estate. Now let's go back to South Bend, Indiana, where the median household income is around $46,610, but the average listing price for a home is $92,138. The average family can afford to buy an average home. That means you have a much broader percentage of the population that can buy your product. Make no mistake: If you're a realtor, San Francisco is the place for you since you work on a commission and you're not out any capital if a house doesn't sell. But as a speculator, mid-size cities are going to be your stock in trade.

There are some cities that are just "on fire," as the real estate agents say. As of January 2016, according to Realtor.com, the hottest real estate markets in the U.S. are:

1. San Francisco, CA

2. San Jose, CA

3. Dallas, TX

4. Vallejo, CA

5. San Diego, CA

6. Sacramento, CA

7. Nashville, TN

8. Stockton, CA

9. Denver, CO

10. Los Angeles, CA

11. Santa Rosa, CA

12. Oxnard, CA

13. Palm Bay, FL

14. Yuba City, CA

15. Modesto, CA

16. Detroit, MI

17. Midland, TX

18. Santa Cruz, CA

19. Tampa, FL

20. Fort Wayne, IN

If you were fortunate enough to purchase real estate in most of these cities a few years ago, you could probably cash in now and retire. But in communities like these, you will hear a lot of hype about the phenomenal growth rates and arguments for "getting in now while you still can." But the problem is, these growth rates will not continue indefinitely. At the high end especially, as the middle class gets pushed out, you will come up against a brick wall when you try to make deals there. When prices get too high, creative financing goes out the window and the barrier to entry gets steep.

So which markets are ideal for real estate investors?

To answer that critical question, *Forbes* magazine partnered with North Carolina-based Local Market Monitor to analyze market conditions in more than 300 markets, ultimately producing a list of the "Best Buy Cities" for 2016. These cities can all boast of strong job growth, population growth, and home price growth. Importantly, most are still deemed "undervalued," which means they have plenty of room to appreciate before they become too risky for investors.

The top markets are:

1. Grand Rapids, MI
2. Orlando, FL
3. San Antonio, TX
4. Charlotte, NC
5. Salt Lake City, UT
6. Dallas, TX
7. Austin, TX
8. Fort Lauderdale, FL
9. Seattle, WA
10. Cape Coral, FL

11. Indianapolis, IN

12. North Port, FL

13. Nashville, TN

14. Tampa, FL

15. Charleston, SC

16. Denver, CO

17. Madison, WI

18. Jacksonville, FL

19. West Palm Beach, FL

20. Boise, ID

WHY SLOW GROWTH COMMUNITIES ARE BETTER INVESTMENTS

On the other hand, the majority of metropolitan communities across America that show much more modest growth in terms of housing prices will have opportunities. The buying opportunities that will allow you to buy distressed properties at low cost and sometimes with no money down are going to be in these communities almost exclusively. Homes will be on the market longer and to your advantage as they will be easier for you to buy. Once you acquire them and renovate if you choose, you can offer them on terms to make them sell faster than the market. You will reap a greater than average profit.

Here's a profitable basic strategy:

1. Buy a home that has been on the market for a long time at a discounted price.

2. Do your renovation.

3. Offer the home for sale on a land contract or "subject to" contract, with an affordable down payment, at 10 to 20 percent above market price, to a good candidate with lower-than-average credit. Charge 3 to 5 percent above the prevailing mortgage interest rate.

WHO'S GOING TO BUY?

Who is a good candidate as a buyer? Ideally, it will be someone who has the dream of homeownership but is credit impaired and may not have a down payment, and therefore does not qualify for traditional bank mortgages.

If you are selling homes in San Francisco, most working people will be completely out of the picture. You will be selling to the wealthy, and they will be more demanding of you and very particular about the property.

Many investors use the logic of selling only to individuals with perfect credit, but you're making the mistake there of thinking like a bank. You're not a bank. You're a real estate investor. You're not selling mortgages. You're selling homes. You're selling a dream. Here's why selling a home to a credit-impaired individual is going to work out best for all concerned: You may be turning a renter into a homeowner. You are helping an individual fulfill a dream. That person is not likely to default on you or skip out. Renters are more likely to skip out, not take care of the property, and make late payments. For this reason, some investors with multiple homes prefer to not rent out any at all, instead offering very easy land contract, "subject to" lease option or rent-to-own deals, often with little or no money down, for the sole purpose of gaining a more dedicated occupant who will take better care of the property.

$$$ *Part-Time Real Estate Investor Tip* $$$

There's nothing wrong with being a landlord. It can be profitable, but when you rent a home to somebody, you're giving them a roof over their head and nothing more. They have little incentive to care for your property. But if you offer them a different sort of contract and allow them to purchase the home directly from you on creative terms and with an affordable down payment, you gain several advantages: First, the burden of maintenance and repair shifts to the occupants. Second, the occupants have a greater incentive to care for the property because they have a stake in its equity. And third, because you are holding the mortgage yourself, you still retain control over the property.

If you can get over the preconceived notion of "sterling credit," you'll always come out ahead. Keep in mind that buying and selling lots of properties on easy terms usually involves distressed properties, fixer-uppers, and marginal neighborhoods. If your buyers had sterling credit and plenty of money, they probably would not be looking at those types of homes.

There's a very good reason that subprime lending has become such a big business in America, and that's simply because millions of Americans have subprime credit. Having subprime credit does not make an individual unworthy. Many banks, mortgage companies, and lenders are making billions of dollars offering "second chance loans," high-risk lines of credit, and no-qualify payday loans to people that are credit-impaired. If it were not profitable, the largest banks and financial institutions in America would not be making these loans — but they are. You gain in several ways: You get to charge a higher price at a greater interest rate, you get a dedicated and grateful customer, and you still have control over the asset. It's win-win, and you can't lose out following this strategy.

CHAPTER 6

Buying Your First Home

T he first one is always the hardest, and the deal will probably be a little different from later ones. You may not make as much money on that first deal as you will later, but that's not the point of your first deal, which is to plant yourself firmly in the real estate business. Make yourself a basic deal on which you can build other deals.

BUYING A HOME TO OCCUPY

If your first deal will be a home you plan to live in, you have a lot more options at your disposal and more flexibility as well. You will likely find the financing much easier. The home my wife and I live in now is a very large historic Victorian built in 1888. We bought it with no money down on creative terms. I wouldn't have bought it as an investment for immediate resale, because it wasn't selling at significantly below market price, but it really is an investment:

- Purchasing this home to live in allows me to take the home interest deduction and save a significant amount of money on my taxes.

- Owning such a home gives me credibility as a businessperson and real estate investor. If you yourself are still renting, nobody is going to take you seriously as a real estate investor. That's why your first investment, if you don't own a home already, *must* be to buy one for yourself.

- The purchase allows me to accumulate equity, which I can leverage later to buy additional homes.

- The purchase allows me to improve the property, which will increase the value and add to equity, which I can leverage later to buy additional homes.

$$$ Part-Time Real Estate Investor Tip $$$

Many people have found success and profit with the "buy, inhabit, rehabilitate, and sell" strategy. By living in a home while you renovate it, you are able to take advantage of programs for homeowner/occupants that are not available to conventional investors. This strategy also relieves you of some of the time pressure you may otherwise face, and you will be free to work at your renovation at a pace that suits your schedule.

FIRST INVESTMENT

When you are making your first real estate investment deal, you haven't established a lot of credibility yet. Nonetheless, there are still multiple ways to go about acquiring your first property:

1. **Creative financing.** Never discount the power of creative financing and doing an end-run around the mortgage lender. You will get better at this with future deals, and as you acquire more, you will have more creative options open to you.

2. **Leverage existing equity of your personal residence.** This is, as they say in the lending business, "putting some of your own skin in the game," and conventional financiers like this approach.

3. **Bank/mortgage lender financing.** Not always a possibility if you don't have some existing equity or other capital.

4. **Third party investor.** Unlikely until you have established a track record as a real estate investor or you are lucky enough to have a rich relative who likes you.

While no-money-down deals are always attractive, and it's almost always good to try to go into a deal with as little up-front capital as possible, your first deal may not always work out this way. Be prepared to put whatever you have on the line.

Keep in mind that you are becoming an entrepreneur, and this means taking a risk. If you're not willing to take a risk, this isn't the business for you, and you should probably go out and get a job at the post office. Keeping in mind that the notion of "security" is an illusion, you must now come to accept the possibility of doing things a little differently.

$$$ *Part-Time Real Estate Investor Tip* $$$

Most of the dot-com millionaires I met and did business with while living in the Silicon Valley area didn't get that way because they had large amounts of money to begin with. They got that way because they put everything they had on the line. One in particular still stands out in my mind because of his story of how he financed his dot-com company. He told people: "I financed my company through a consortium of international banks." This line was true but not quite as it seemed. In reality, the consortium consisted of every single bank that was willing to provide him with a credit card. He put everything on the line, maxed out all of his credit cards, and went into debt. He was able to turn that extremely risky strategy into millions of dollars.

Many people spend their lives doing two things: slowly accumulating wealth through equity, savings, pensions and retirement accounts; and avoiding debt. These individuals would sooner cut off a finger than dip into their savings or max out a credit card. All of their lives, they have had the notion of security drummed into their heads and have come to believe that certain things are just never done for any reason. These are not people who are going to make a lot of investments aside from government bonds. For people who are not entrepreneurs (real estate or otherwise), this is a fine approach. But for you, who want to make big profits, you must be willing to put that notion aside.

If you have equity in your home, you must leverage it and be prepared to borrow against it. If you have credit cards or can get them, be prepared to use them to obtain cash or purchase your renovation supplies. If you can get a line of credit from the bank because you have a good day job, sign up for it. Life insurance policies, retirement accounts, personal savings, and stocks and bonds you may have are all fair game. Nothing is sacred. You must be a gambler, but with some inside knowledge of the house's system.

FIRST DEAL PROFITS

It happens frequently that smart people get caught up in the excitement and hype of becoming a real estate investor. They focus on the "deal," and on acquiring the property as quickly as possible through creative means and amaze themselves that they are able to make such deals that require very little money down, or ones that they thought they would never be able to pull off.

But there's one problem: When you focus so much on the deal itself, and get caught up in the excitement of negotiation and deal-making, it's very possible to lose sight of your goal — which is to turn a profit. It seems like an obvious thing to keep in mind, but surprisingly, even intelligent people lose sight of it. Making real estate deals is addictive, and in a way, is its own reward. It's fun to do. But at the end of the day, you want to have more money in your pocket than when you started out.

Two things to remember above all, aside from all the creative techniques, are:

1. Crunch your numbers on every permutation of the deal; and

2. Plan for contingencies.

That is to say, a deal may look very good on paper, but that paperwork assumes that the property will be turned around quickly. But what if that doesn't happen? Do you have enough money to carry it on your own? Talk to some real estate people who specialize in the area in which you are buying and try to take note yourself of how long properties stay on the market. You may be allowing yourself two months to do renovations, but you may also need to allow for another six months for the property to sell. If your research shows that properties stay on the market an average of six months in the area, build six months of payments into your profit calculations.

The final price is actually less important than the ratio of the amount of actual cash you have to put out to what you anticipate to bring in. Unless you're an all-cash buyer, which is unlikely, you aren't putting out $100,000 for a $100,000 house. Let's look at a deal:

Let's say you buy a house for $100,000 on a land contract, with 5 percent down and 9 percent interest. Principal and interest payments are $764.39, and let's assume that taxes and insurance bring your monthly expenses to $900. Now let's say your plan is to fix it up and re-sell it for a profit. Homes usually stay on the market in the area for six months, and that will give you plenty of time to do the renovations you have planned. Now let's budget another $5,000 for renovations. After six months, you will have put out a total of $15,400. Don't make the mistake of thinking, "I just spent $100,000 for an investment house." You didn't. You spent $15,400 for an investment house.

Now after six months, you have $5,317.24 in equity. Subtract that from your $15,400 that you've spent, and you are still down $10,082.76. The longer the house sits on the market, the more interest you are paying on your land contract loan. True, you are also gaining equity, but you are gaining very little equity during the first couple years of a mortgage. Now if you are able to sell that home for $115,000 to a cash buyer, you can pay off your loan, reimburse yourself for your renovations, and still come out with a profit:

Cash in from sale:	115,000
Pay off loan	94,682
Interest paid for six months	4,269
Taxes/Insurance for six months	814
Renovation expenses	5,000
Less down payment	5,000
Profit:	**5,235**

Now let's look at the percentages. You're making a $5,235 profit from a $100,000 house, so you may think you're getting about a 5 percent return. But in reality, it's much more. You've only spent $15,400, and you're getting back $5,235, so your percentage return is 33 percent over six months. Annualize that and you're getting a return of 66 percent per annum. A lot more than you'd ever get from a bank!

While the price you pay is obviously important, equally important is:

- The amount of interest you are paying while you are holding the note

- How long the property sits empty

- How much you spend on renovation

Any one of these three factors, if they aren't planned for correctly, can make the difference between profit and loss. As such, you want to negotiate your deal so that you are paying the least amount of interest possible every month on your note. Structuring a deal so that your monthly payments are actually larger but the interest is lower (assuming that you can support the payments in the interim) will yield you a greater profit at the end of the deal.

This is why later on, after you have made a few deals and have accumulated a cash stockpile, you will make money faster. You will be able to make more powerful offers with larger payments and lower interest, and your profit margin will increase over time. Keep this in mind when you are first starting out: Your profit margin on your first few deals may be a little subpar, but this is to be expected because your negotiating power is not yet strong. But don't let that stop you; just keep going and it will improve.

$$$ *Part-Time Real Estate Investor Tip* $$$

Set a goal for return on your investment. In real estate it is quite reasonable to be able to expect a 50 percent annual return on your money. If you start out with a $10,000 investment, you can do some simple math and see that you can snowball that into a cool million in about 12 years.

COMMON FIRST DEAL MISTAKES

As I've said here, almost anybody can make a real estate deal. Not everybody can make a good one. There are many books and programs that vow "real estate is a sure thing," but in reality, it isn't. It's a good thing, and given the right attention to detail and diligence on the part of the investor, you can make money. But it's not a sure thing. There is no sure thing. There are no guarantees. There is no security. "All things are impermanent." A lot of people make money in real estate, but there are still people who don't. A little common sense and attention to detail will yield you a profit. Avoid common mistakes that beginners often make, and you can get rich.

Here are some of the most common mistakes made by beginning real estate investors.

1. *Focus too much on the "no-money-down" deal.* This is truly an exciting way to buy property, and often a good way. But when you're investing in real estate, the more options to have at your disposal, the better off you will be.

2. *Put too much time and effort into a single deal.* Trading a dozen middle-class homes will almost always yield better results, and produce less risk than putting all your resources into a single, larger property.

3. *Try to do too many deals, too quickly.* This is especially important in your first few deals. Once you have your first project under way, you will start to see a lot more. Avoid the temptation to take on as many as you can get your hands on, and wait until you have your first deal completed — bought, renovated, sold, and money in your pocket — until you take on a second. After you've done a couple, then start juggling an increasing number of deals simultaneously.

4. *Making the deal at any cost.* This mistake is more common among those investors who are credit impaired or have little capital. There are deals you can get with bad credit and no capital, but they are not all good deals. Do the math and make sure there will be profit at the end of the day.

5. *Forget that there is no such thing as security.* Always remember this fact of life. Even in real estate, there is no sure thing, despite what you may have heard in an expensive seminar. Some deals will go bad. If you want to maintain rental properties, sometimes you will get bad tenants. The local market may go bad. Accept the fact that sometimes things will not go your way, but don't let it deter you from making more deals.

CHAPTER 7

Bad Credit

If you have excellent credit, you have a lot of options at your disposal. You will get the best deals possible, low interest rates, and you will be able to qualify very easily for a loan. You will earn greater profits on your real estate deals because your interest expenses will be lower. Available properties will be awaiting you.

But don't make the mistake of thinking you need perfect credit to be a real estate investor. You don't. In fact, you can have the worst credit in the world and still buy real estate. Here's how to do it.

First of all, find out just how bad your credit is and get a copy of your report. While you're working on your real estate business, try to repair your credit to the best of your ability so that future deals will become easier. Then, make a list of your options. One common mistake is to simply apply for mortgages at as many different places as possible; this is a waste of time and also an additional strike against your credit for making too many applications. Another common mistake is to walk into your neighborhood bank—you know, the one that advertises "friendly loan agents who don't like to say no." In fact, they do like to say no, and will probably say it to you. With poor credit, conventional lenders will not give you the time of day, and they will give you some very bad advice. They will tell you to put off trying to buy a home, save money for a 20 percent down payment, spend two or three years cleaning up your credit, and try again. That is very bad advice indeed, because they are telling you to take two or three years out of your real estate business that you are trying desperately to start. That's two or three years that you could be making money, but aren't, because some banker in a suit told you that you couldn't.

You can buy with bad credit, but should you?

Yes, you can. And you should, and as quickly as possible, because real estate investing is one way you can improve your income and your credit at the same time. Don't wait until you have perfect credit to begin. Too many people put off the decision to invest in real estate, or even to buy a home for themselves, because they don't have perfect credit. They are afraid that (1) they won't be able to qualify for anything, and (2) if they do, they will have to pay more.

To address the first point, you can, in fact, qualify with bad credit. And to address the second point, yes, you will have to pay more, but in the long run it may still be worthwhile. High interest shouldn't be a deal-breaker if it's your only option. Keep in mind that if you get a mortgage with high interest, that mortgage doesn't have to persist for 30 years. After a few years, your credit score may improve, and you will have gained equity in the property (which you can use as leverage for additional loans), and you can refinance it at a lower interest rate.

$$$ *Part-Time Real Estate Investor Tip* $$$

Don't wait. Even if you have bad credit, dive right in as soon as you possibly can. Those who wait for every condition to be perfect often end up with nothing.

That said, be aware that without good credit, your options are limited. That doesn't mean you have no options; it just means that you have fewer of them. Cash is king, and if you have lots of cash, people will listen. You can buy anything, and you will get the best deals and greater profits. If you can purchase your property with 100 percent cash, your credit report is completely irrelevant. But we all must work with what we have available.

There are two things to take away from this chapter: (1) start as soon as possible regardless of your credit, and (2) improve your credit so you will have more options open to you. If you have bad credit, there are a lot of properties that could be very profitable investments that will be completely unavailable to you. Don't despair. There are still deals you can make and properties you can purchase, so you should work within the available parameters. In the meantime, improve your credit and accumulate assets so you can prepare for the future.

IMPROVING YOUR CREDIT

I advocate jumping right in and buying your first investment property as soon as you can, even if you have abysmal credit. You will pay more in interest and fees, but at least you will be able to get your start. However, while you are getting your feet wet making deals and acquiring wealth, you must also work on improving your credit at the same time. That's because, as I've said earlier, it's better to have more options. If you have terrible credit, you have a relative handful of ways you can buy a piece of property, and the pool of properties that are available to you is very small. But if you have good credit, you have more ways to buy and a greater pool of properties available to you. So get started now and work with what you have available, but at the same time, improve your prospects for the future. This year, with bad credit, maybe you will be able to buy two or three pieces of real estate and make your first profits. In three years, with excellent credit, you may be buying 200 or more.

PARTNERS

One of the techniques that they present in the real estate seminars and in the "no-money-down" books is to use OPM, or "other peoples' money." And if you can pull it off, it's great. The technique is simply to get a private investor/lender to put up the money you need to make your deal, and then either share the profits with the investor or repay the lender at a high rate of interest.

However, this isn't as easy as it sounds. The real estate gurus tout this technique as a sure thing, since you can offer "investments secured by real estate." The gold ring here is to find an investor willing to make you an interest-bearing loan based on the underlying property, and not your personal credit rating or existing assets. And there are some investors who will bite at that, but not many. Nonetheless, it is one technique that's worth trying out.

Many investors who are willing to bankroll your real estate venture will want you to have an established track record as a real estate developer. Even though the deal may be secured by the underlying property, most will refuse to take on such a deal with someone who has never done it before. In addition to experience, the investors are also likely to want more than just monthly payments and interest. They are more likely to want a percent of the profits in addition to a guaranteed return. You may have to give away half the profits and then some. Sharing your profits should always be the avenue of last resort; it's far better to just pay an above-average interest rate and perhaps a fee and reap the larger rewards yourself.

Getting a partner who is willing to bankroll your venture becomes much easier under any of the following conditions:

$$$ *Part-Time Real Estate Investor Tip* $$$

Having cash, equity, or other assets doesn't matter if you have the worst credit in the world. With a high enough down payment, you may even qualify for a "low doc" loan where the lender doesn't even bother to check your credit. Come up with half down, and lenders will be falling over themselves to give you money, even if your FICO score is the lowest they've ever seen.

- You are also putting up capital or assets of your own in addition to the property you want to buy.

- You have experience as a real estate investor/developer.

- You know the investor personally.

Proceed with caution and know ahead of time all the fees and terms you are getting yourself into, but don't rule out subprime lenders if they are your only option. The high interest and fees will cut into your profit, but some profit is better than none. Keep in mind that you can always refinance later. Make sure that the early payoff terms are not too difficult. Some subprime lenders will charge you a hefty fee if you pay off your loan early. Also be aware that you will almost assuredly have to purchase private mortgage insurance (PMI), which will further eat away at your profits.

ALTERNATIVE FINANCING

Alternative financing methods are sometimes not dependent on your credit, and we'll explore the specifics of these techniques in Part Two. Understand that if you have bad credit, or worse—if you have bad credit and no cash—it is going to be hard for you to make a real estate deal. The majority of properties will require you to have good credit, available cash, or both. But those who boast about buying homes with no money down and poor credit realize one thing, and this is where you will separate yourself from the novices: it's all a game of numbers. That is, there is a certain percentage of properties that you will be able to purchase regardless of your credit or available cash. That is a very small percentage, but if you make enough offers, you will occasionally hit one.

Go out and try to buy two or three properties with bad credit, and you'll probably walk away empty-handed. Try to buy a hundred, and you may walk away with one if you're looking in the right places. And that's where your real estate business starts.

BAD CREDIT IS LESS RELEVANT IF YOU'RE BUYING A HOUSE NOBODY WANTS

One important thing to realize is that as an investor, you can profit from buying homes that are substandard, in dodgy neighborhoods, or are just plain ugly. Homes can always be renovated, and sometimes the ugliest home on the block can be made to look like the prettiest with just a little bit of paint and plaster.

When people go out to buy a home to live in, they pay a great deal of attention to how the home looks right then, and naturally, they want to get the most attractive home they can find. But as an investor, you have to turn that around. The most attractive home you can find is going to cost you more money, be harder to acquire, and will yield a smaller profit. The ugly homes you can get for a song, fix up, and sell for a larger profit are the ones you want. And the advantage here is that because the home is ugly, needs repair, and is in a less desirable neighborhood, you can get it on good terms. Often if the home is in this sort of situation, the seller is very anxious to get rid of it. It may have been sitting on the market for several months or even years, and the owner will be a lot more willing to take a creative offer that is not dependent on your credit rating. These are the homes that you can acquire using creative techniques described in Part Two, such as land contract, lease option, "subject to," payment takeover, or even a tax sale.

PART TWO

SPECIFIC STRATEGIES

CHAPTER 8

Land Contract and Lease Purchases

One of the easiest ways to become a successful real estate investor is to become familiar and comfortable with alternative methods of buying and selling. Two types of instruments will be powerful weapons in your arsenal, and you can use these instruments both to acquire and to sell properties.

The first instrument is called a land contract, also known as a "wraparound mortgage" or "contract sale." In short, it is a way a home can be sold or purchased without having to go through a mortgage company. It is a contract that exists between the buyer and seller only, and the buyer makes payments directly to the seller instead of through a mortgage company or bank. If you are selling a home on land contract, you are essentially loaning the buyer the money to buy the property from you and receiving installment payments.

BUYING ON LAND CONTRACT

The most immediate advantage of buying a property with a land contract is that you don't have to meet a mortgage company's qualifications. You do have to meet the individual seller's qualifications, but those tend to be more flexible. A seller offering property on these terms will often be quite lenient and will not even check credit.

Be aware that a land contract is a legal agreement between a buyer and a seller. Among some real estate professionals and bankers, you will find a bias against this type of instrument, primarily because it cuts the real estate professionals and bankers out of the action. They may try to tell you that it is unwise to use this type of instrument, and they may even try to tell you that it is illegal. It is not true. The banking/real estate lobby simply wants to preserve the status quo and believes any deal that does not include them is inherently inferior.

You won't be able to find land contract deals in every city. In high-priced cities where real estate moves quickly, you are unlikely to find one. But in ordinary, working-class cities with working-class homes, they are abundant. You can find sellers willing to sell a house to you on a land contract usually for one of two reasons: either they don't need their equity out of the home immediately and just want a monthly income stream without the hassle of renting, or the house is in poor condition and would be unlikely to sell on conventional terms. Either way, you can turn a profit from such a deal. Buying a home in poor condition isn't always a bad thing to do, and it has become a major source of wealth for many investors who are interested in renovation.

One thing that scares some people away from land contract purchases is that the land contract is always subordinate to any other existing mortgage that may exist. As such, it is less secure. But there is really no such thing as security, no matter what sort of deal you are going into, even if there are banks involved. Sure, there is an element of risk in buying property on this basis. Risk is the basis of entrepreneurship. Don't be afraid to take it.

If you buy a house on land contract, but the seller has an existing underlying mortgage, the way it is supposed to work is that the underlying mortgage payments get paid out of the payments you are making to the seller. But suppose the seller just pockets the money and doesn't make the payments. The seller's mortgage company will foreclose, seize the property, and not acknowledge the existence of the land contract. For this reason, if you have a land contract, it is best to spend a few extra dollars and have all the transactions take place through an escrow company that will simply take your monthly payments, make payments on existing notes, pay the taxes and insurance, and send the balance to the seller every month.

Alternately, you can take over these responsibilities yourself, sending out multiple checks instead of just one every month. Don't worry about sending a check to a mortgage company for a mortgage that is in the name of the seller. So long as the mortgage company is getting a check on a timely basis, they really don't care where it's coming from. If you do get into a fix where a bank is foreclosing on a land contract property, it's important to try to be proactive and know when the seller is getting into trouble and know where those underlying mortgages are. That way you can establish contact with the note-holder right away, because it's not likely that that they will go out of their way to contact you, since they may not even be aware that a land contract exists. If the bank is foreclosing on the property, and you can go in and tell them you have a land contract and have been making timely payments all along, they may be willing to cut you a deal and let you assume the mortgage. Of course, there are no guarantees that they will do so, and they have no legal obligation to you whatsoever. But, if you make things easy for them, if you've been making regular payments and can prove it, and if you can sweeten the pot with a cash down payment, they are much more likely to let you take it over (or write you a new mortgage) as opposed to going through the hassle and expense of foreclosure.

Making a land contract offer gives you a lot of flexibility and a lot more negotiating room than you otherwise would have. The seller is not bound by any corporate guidelines or banking rules; how you structure the deal is strictly between the buyer and seller alone. Structure your offer so that you are bringing something desirable to the table to convince the seller to make the deal, but also make it easy on yourself. Find out what the seller is looking for. Most of the time, a land contract seller is looking for one or more of the following:

- Up-front cash to take care of personal bills.

- Freedom from landlord responsibilities such as maintenance.

- A reliable monthly check.

- To sell a property that would not sell on conventional terms.

Understanding which of those things the seller wants will help you structure an acceptable offer. If the house needs a substantial amount of cosmetic fix-up for example, structure your offer so that you put down a very small or no down payment at all, but take on all responsibilities for ongoing maintenance, repair and renovation, and accept the property on an "as-is" basis.

You will find two different types of sellers when you are seeking to buy on land contract: individuals who fit into one of the above desired categories, and individuals who are investors like yourself. You will find the better deals when buying from sellers who have a few properties as a sideline or just want to sell their primary residence rather than buying from another investor. The reasons will become obvious in the next section.

SELLING ON LAND CONTRACT

Selling homes on land contract terms can also be very profitable for you. Even though you won't get all your money at once when you sell on these terms, you still get some big advantages.

As an alternative to being a landlord, selling on land contract brings you the monthly income stream that you would get from running rental properties, but you are relieved of many of the hassles and you will get better quality people in your homes because the people living in your homes are not just tenants; they are buyers themselves. They will care more about the property than would a renter and are much more likely to stay long-term and fulfill the terms of their contract. Also, because they are buyers, your normal landlord duties, such as fixing broken furnaces and replacing old refrigerators, are gone. And if you are unfortunate enough to live in a community with strict rent control laws (which make being a landlord unprofitable), those laws won't apply to you since you are not a landlord.

When you are selling a property on land contract, realize that the people who want to buy from you are probably not rich people. They are likely to have impaired credit and little money to put down. But don't let that deter you from making a deal. You are giving these individuals a big incentive to take care of the property and to perform on their mortgage note to you, since you are giving them a break that the bank would never consider giving.

Maintaining a strict application process and requiring perfect credit is likely to eliminate almost all of your potential customers. At the same time, it is important to screen your customers and gather some information. Be willing to work with people with bad credit, but gain some knowledge of their work situation and income. If possible, arrange for payments to be made to you electronically through automatic debit.

This situation naturally gives you the upper hand in negotiation. For this reason, you can almost always sell the house for or above market value. At the same time, however, make sure you structure the payments so that you are getting profit every month but the payment is still affordable to the customer. In terms of the deal itself, you are writing a mortgage between yourself and the buyer, and you can write it however you want. Usually a seller will charge an interest rate that is above what would normally be charged by a conventional lender by at least two or three points, sometimes much more. If the current rate being offered by mortgage companies to their best customers is 6 percent, you should charge at least 9 percent.

Think about your return both in short-term and long-term. In the short-term, make sure you are getting enough each month to cover all your expenses (underlying mortgage, taxes, and insurance), and provide you with a monthly profit. In the long-term, make sure you are getting an above-market return on your investment.

Most land contracts have a "balloon" clause. That is, the note is written on a standard 30-year term for the purpose of calculating the monthly payment, but the note becomes due after a certain period of time, such as three to five years. This allows you the option of calling the note after a predetermined time. This time also gives your buyers a reasonable amount of time to improve their own credit to the point where they can qualify for a conventional mortgage at a lower rate of interest. If your buyers are unable to pay off the note to you when the balloon clause comes due, then they default and the property reverts to you. The terms of the balloon are always flexible, and you are free to negotiate with your buyer so terms can meet both your needs. A one-year balloon is usually inadequate, although some less scrupulous investors use it simply as a way to force tenants into default and cause them to lose their down payments. In the long run, though, you will come out better by crafting terms that your buyers are likely to be able to meet. If your buyers want time to improve their credit and get a conventional mortgage, one year is just not enough time to do that. A fairly crafted balloon clause is good for both parties: your buyer gets an opportunity to buy out your note at a lower interest rate later on and you get an opportunity to cash in your equity and take all your profit within a reasonable amount of time.

THE LEASE PURCHASE

A lease purchase contract, sometimes called a lease purchase agreement, deals aren't usually considered ways to acquire real estate, but occasionally they can work to your advantage, or at least help you get your foot in the door when you are just starting out. You are limited in this deal, however. Since it is not a purchase, you cannot re-sell the property, but (subject to the terms of the lease, anyway) you can rent it out.

A lease purchase is a document that is really just a lease, but a certain percentage of your lease payments is applied toward an eventual purchase or down payment. Down payment or deposit is usually also applied to purchase. At the end of the lease term, you will have built up equity in the property, and can then use that toward a purchase. Indeed, such transactions are often referred to as a lease with an option to purchase.

If you are acquiring a property in this way, one of the most important things is the amount of your lease payment that applies to purchase. Some owners may offer only a token amount; as an investor you want to have as much of your payment apply toward purchase as possible. At the very least, the amount that applies to purchase should be equal to the amount of equity you would build up if you were purchasing the property. You can easily calculate this with any mortgage calculator. Suppose the property is valued at $100,000, and you have a lease purchase with a term of two years. Over that 24 months, if you were to obtain a 30-year mortgage for $100,000 at 7 percent, you would acquire equity totaling $2,105. Divide this figure by 24, and you can calculate that your lease purchase should be crediting you a minimum of $87 a month toward your eventual purchase.

There is a particular technique here that you should never use if you are trying to acquire property on lease purchase, but you can use it yourself if you are trying to sell on lease purchase. In this technique, the seller figures the market rental rate for the property. Suppose, for example, that if the home were to be offered as a straight rental, it would yield $900 a month. The seller then offers it at $1,000 a month, and credits the buyer with $100 a month toward purchase. You can see that all the advantage here is given to the seller, and the buyer gets very little except an eventual opportunity to buy a house. The buyer is just as well off renting during the period, and placing $100 a month in an interest-bearing savings account.

As a buyer, though, a lease option buys you time. If the home needs some substantial repair, for example, it can be a good instrument for you to work on it for a couple years and increase the property's value, while locking in a price. Keep in mind, though, that a lease option is still just a lease, and although the sellers are required by the contract to keep their end of the bargain after the term, your claim on the property in the interim period is still tenuous.

If you acquire a property in this manner, make sure to visit your local courthouse and file a "memorandum of option" or "lien of interest" after you sign the deal. This will help to give legal "teeth" to your right to purchase the property on the terms stated when the lease is ended.

CHAPTER 9

Buying Investment Property with No Money Down

Following the "no-money-down" techniques are useful and can make an excellent way to get your foot in the door of the real estate investment world. But you should by no means limit yourself to these techniques once you've started. After making your first few deals, you will have more credibility, better credit, more assets, and more cash in hand, and you will have a lot more techniques at your disposal. While no-money-down deals will work sometimes and under certain circumstances, cash *always* works.

$$$ *Part-Time Real Estate Investor Tip* $$$

One thing to be aware of with no-money-down deals is that they tend to make your monthly maintenance expense higher. When calculating your monthly payment, the larger your down payment, the smaller the monthly payment—and so when your down payment is zero, your monthly payment is naturally going to be larger. Before you embark on a no-money-down" deal, make sure you can handle the larger monthly payment and that you will still earn a profit. If you are planning to rent out the property, make sure that the market rate for rent exceeds your monthly payment plus other maintenance expenses.

In general, real estate seminars, books and get-rich-quick schemes focus way too much on the "no-money-down" aspect of real estate investing. Yes, it can be done, and if you're broke, it may be the only option open to you.

But the more techniques you have, the better your deals will be, the more deals you can make, and the richer you will become.

The low-hanging fruit of the no-money-down deal is based on either your excellent credit or on your existing equity or assets you have somewhere else. It's relatively easy to get a house with no money down if you have the best credit in the world, or if you have a million bucks in the bank already. That's why later on in your business, once you have made deals and accumulated some wealth, it gets easier. Ironically, no-money-down deals become a lot more possible when you no longer need them. However, there are still some possibilities for those who do.

There is almost no chance of a no-money-down deal when you are talking about conventional financing. There are some types of financing where you can minimize your down payment. If you have excellent credit, you may be able to qualify for a mortgage with 5 percent down. The FHA has some programs where your down payment may be as low as 3 percent, but no bank is going to let you off the hook completely. Take heart. There are still ways to nail down a no-money-down home. Here are some techniques:

Land contract or "wraparound mortgage"

As outlined in the previous chapter, a land contract is a private instrument between a buyer and a seller. Because it does not involve banks or mortgage companies, the terms are completely flexible and a seller will often be willing to sell it to you for no money down. This is not always the case though, and it depends largely on the sellers' financial situation, as well as the condition of the property and the marketplace itself. If the sellers have a property they desperately need to walk away from, they may well be in need of some cash (for example, to pay off bills or to bring their mortgage up to date), and a no-money-down deal will not solve their problems. But if they are up to date on their mortgage and just need to get out from under it, no-money-down may be a possibility for them, especially if the property is in a distressed area, needs repair, or is in an area where the real estate market is exceptionally soft.

Lease purchase

Also discussed in the previous chapter, lease purchase is one that won't often work, but once in a while it will work to your advantage if you can arrange payment terms that are advantageous to you. If the property is in good condition and in a desirable neighborhood, no-money-down is not likely to be a possibility. But if a seller is anxious to make a deal and there is no immediate prospect of a sale, a lease purchase with no down payment may well be an offer worth considering. Make the offer with no money down, and make sure to include in your offer all the details of the amount from each monthly payment that will get credited toward your purchase.

"Subject to"

A variation of the land contract—a "subject to" contract—is one where you make payments on the seller's mortgage. Existing financing remains in place, and your claim is "subject to" that underlying financing. You take the seller's payment book and make the payments yourself. If the seller has some equity, you may also need to make monthly payments to the seller as well.

This is a deal that, like most no-money-down deals, doesn't always work, but when it does, it's wonderful. It is usually dependent on several conditions coming together: You must find a homeowner who no longer wants their home, usually because they can no longer afford the payments or the upkeep. They want out of their mortgage right away and are probably in some financial distress, perhaps at risk of foreclosure. The local market is usually soft so that selling the home through conventional means must be problematic for the seller. They want out, and they want out now, and you are their only option other than just walking away and defaulting.

In this case, the homeowner's advantage is that they avoid foreclosure and are able to walk away immediately without harming their credit any more than they have already. Their risk is that you will not perform on their mortgage—in which case they will still be held liable. As such, this requires the homeowner to trust you.

Assuming that those conditions have been met and you have a willing (and possibly desperate) seller, you must then assess the property itself and determine whether you can turn a profit on it. Assuming you can put some work into it and make it presentable without too large an investment, you may be able to turn it into a money-producing rental fairly quickly, or even sell it at a profit, pay off your distressed seller's mortgage completely, and pocket the difference.

Leverage credit cards

If you have no money but have a wallet full of high-value credit cards, don't discount their value. Sure, you will hear that you should keep your credit card balance low, and obviously there is a risk of getting into trouble with too much unsecured credit card debt. But at the same time, it can be a source of funds. The interest rate is likely to be exceedingly high, but you can still leverage your available credit card funds to get what you need to get into a house.

Understand that this won't work with a conventional lender. You will not be able to borrow a down payment off your credit cards to make up the down payment on a conventional mortgage. But you can do that if you are working directly with a seller (for example, on a land contract). Or if the property is cheap enough and you have enough available credit on your cards, it could even be possible to fund the entire purchase price solely on credit cards.

Of course, the interest may make the deal prohibitive, but here's what you can do about that: Since you have purchased the house using unsecured credit, you now own the house free and clear, even though you are in debt up to your eyeballs for it. That's because unlike a mortgage, which takes the property as security, your credit cards do not require security. You can now take out a mortgage on the house that you now own, and use the proceeds to pay off your credit cards. You are therefore able to trade a lower-rate mortgage for your higher-rate credit cards, and you will have only paid the high credit card interest rate for a short period of time.

Leverage existing equity in other homes

Once you've made a few deals, you will have a chance to accumulate some equity in your homes, and you can use this to bankroll subsequent deals. Once you have several properties with equity, a bank is likely to be willing to give you a loan against your equity, which you can use to acquire more property. There are two ways this can happen: The bank may wish to approve a loan for you simply using all of your existing properties as collateral, or you can get a loan using a specific piece of property. Avoid using all your property for any single loan if possible, as a step to isolate the risk. If a deal goes really bad, it is better to lose one property as opposed to all of them.

Two mortgages (80-20)

This one works if you have excellent credit; and by "excellent," I mean absolutely the best credit possible. Otherwise the lender would never allow it. The deal works like this: You take out two mortgages, one for 80 percent, and one for 20 percent. The 20 percent mortgage is subordinate to the 80 percent one, and therefore carries a high rate of interest. The 80 percent loan carries the normal interest rate. Not all banks and lenders offer programs like this, but look around.

Alternately, you can get an 80 percent mortgage and ask the seller to carry a second mortgage for 20 percent directly. Several conditions have to be right for this to work: The seller must have 20 percent equity in the property to be able to do this; and both seller and lender must agree.

ASK FOR THE BEST DEAL

You never know unless you ask. Buying property with no money down is mostly showmanship and having enough guts to ask for something you don't have any right to get. But sometimes you get lucky.

When my wife and I found the 120-year-old Victorian home of our dreams, the asking price was $115,000. The seller was willing to execute a land contract with a three-year balloon term with $5,000 down—very reasonable, but not good enough for me. The house was in an "emerging" neighborhood that was still a bit dodgy, and there were still some renovations to be made. I asked for and received three things.

The first thing I asked for and received was a five-year balloon instead of the three. Easy enough. But the seller knew that it was just a bit over budget for me. I wanted something with payments of around $900 a month; the land contract terms with interest and taxes would bring the payment up to over $1,200 a month. "That's a deal-breaker," I said, honestly explaining that I don't want to get into a situation where monthly payments are too difficult. The seller appreciated the candor and offered a solution: Pay her the $900 a month, and the difference would accumulate and be due at the end of the term or on completion of sale. Last, I explained my plans for renovation in detail and explained how much I would be spending on them. Then I asked for the gold: "no money down." Because I would be making significant repairs and renovations—and if for some reason I defaulted, the seller would reap the benefit of those renovations. She agreed.

In this case, I asked for something that I knew I would be unlikely to receive, but I did receive it because of three things: I spoke with confidence, outlined a workable plan, and offered value to the seller. I did go on to spend thousands of dollars on renovations, and this in itself provided the seller with the needed reassurance and the added value of knowing that if I defaulted, she would get back the property in an improved state.

CHAPTER 10

Foreclosures and REO Properties

One of the most exciting and potentially most profitable areas of real estate investment you will find is in buying foreclosures.

Before I get into the details, let's talk about the 800-pound gorilla in the room that everybody wants to avoid. Yes, when you become a foreclosure investor, you are in the business of making money because somebody else has lost or is losing their home. It's a zero-sum game. For you to win, somebody else has to lose. If this bothers you from a karmic or spiritual point of view, then don't do it. But one thing to realize is that you are not the one doing the foreclosing. You are just the one who wants to buy the property from the party who did. Second, in some cases you will actually be doing the homeowner a service, depending on how you go about it.

Why are there foreclosures?

Homeownership has become easier in part due to changes in government policies. There are many more homeowners today than 20 years ago, and just because of the sheer numbers involved, a certain number of homeowners are not going to be able to make it. Maybe the person being foreclosed on has lost a job, suffered an illness, or the loss of an income-producing family member. Maybe they just spent too much on other things and can't pay their bills. Whatever the reason, it happens everywhere in America.

To be sure, there are fewer foreclosures now than during the real estate meltdown of 2008. According to RealtyTrac, just 1 in 13,000 homes ends up in foreclosure. The states in which foreclosures were most common in 2016 were Maryland and New Jersey. In those states, about 1 in every 550 homes ends up in foreclosure. And that can spell opportunity.

Lenders are typically willing to unload these properties at attractive prices. They usually just want to break even with an asking price that's often the sum of the remaining mortgage plus interest, lawyer fees, and penalties. The price ends up being about 15 percent below the actual value of the property.

Foreclosures can be tremendous opportunities for people who aggressively pursue them. But it's worth remembering that you may run into lots of competition these days. Investors are not the only ones seeking out such deals. People interested in purchasing a residence have also discovered this market, so stay on your toes.

THE FORECLOSURE PROCESS

It is important to know a little about the process so you can profit from it. Foreclosure doesn't happen overnight, and it can be a long process. Banks will typically offer a homeowner workaround opportunities, even after the initial notice has been given. The legal process varies from state to state.

Generally, what happens is a lender first delivers the homeowner delinquency notices and attempts to collect the past due amount, sometimes offering payment plans and other options. Depending on the lender, a "notice of default" is delivered much later. A subprime lender will be quicker to act, foreclosing on people who are as little as 30 days behind, but most banks will wait several months before taking this step. A notice of default is a legal notice, which is often published in the legal ad section of the newspaper. Again, once the notice of default has been given, the lender may wait anywhere between one month and six months before a foreclosure sale takes place, depending on the laws of the state and individual circumstances.

The law does afford the homeowner several remedies, and the process can be time consuming. So if you have your eye on a piece of property that's still in the foreclosure process, you may have a long wait. But, when it's through, the property is sold off to the highest bidder. In some cases, this may be you. Often, the lender winds up owning the property outright after the auction if nobody bids high enough. This is what's known as an REO (real-estate-owned) property.

$$$ *Part-Time Real Estate Investor Tip* $$$

Even after you've made your bid, had it accepted, and you gain title to the property, it sometimes happens that there are still people living in the house who have no right to be there. If the property had been vacant, squatters may be there, in which case you bring the sheriff with you to remove them from the property physically. Sometimes, the former homeowners are still there and may stand their ground and try any number of delaying tactics, sympathy ploys, or legal maneuvers. Once you have won your bid and have the title in your hands, whoever is in there loses their rights to the property, but they can still cause you unnecessary delays.

Once a foreclosure takes place, all liens that are inferior to the primary one will be eliminated to the extent that there is no money left after the first lien has been paid. For example: Suppose you buy a house at auction for $50,000. There was a first mortgage with an outstanding balance of $45,000 and a second mortgage of $10,000. The first mortgage holder would get their entire $45,000, but the second lien holder would get only $5,000, and you would have no obligation to pay off the rest.

PENNIES ON THE DOLLAR

Those that are not familiar with real estate believe that people can make a killing by buying foreclosures for "pennies on the dollar" and then selling the homes at full market value or renting them out. This isn't how it works. When a bank takes possession of a home, it's true that it's not in their best interest to hang onto it. They want to get it off their portfolio. But, that doesn't mean they are going to give it away at bargain basement prices. There are several myths that float around concerning how banks handle properties they own. They are not going to sell it for just enough to cover their losses, and they are not going to sell it for just the balance due. When a bank sells a property they have foreclosed on, they are allowed by law to make a profit on it, over and above any losses they may have incurred as a result of the foreclosure. And while some banks sell their REOs directly, others sell them through realtors, making the price even higher, since the realtor's commission is then figured into the deal.

Having said that, the bank realizes that they have a nonperforming asset and they will be willing to sell it to you at a discount, simply because to the bank owning a piece of real estate instead of owning a *mortgage* on a piece of real estate doesn't make them any money. As such, there is an opportunity cost that they must bear. Banks make money on money. Having money tied up in a piece of real estate means there is that much less they have to lend out, and so they are actually suffering a dual loss: first from the loss of a paying mortgage holder, and second, from having a non-productive asset tying up their money. And *that's* why they sell their foreclosures at a discount. They do have some very precise calculations they use to figure out just how much money they are losing, and the price they set is precisely calculated.

$$$ *Part-Time Real Estate Investor Tip* $$$

Foreclosed properties listed through real estate agents will give you limited profits. Listed deals like this make money for the agent first and you second. Find banks and lenders that sell their REOs directly for the greatest flexibility.

HOW TO FIND FORECLOSURES AND REOS

The internet will be your greatest resources when it comes to hunting these potential properties. Many free resources are available, so be wary of anyone offering to sell you a list.

A great place to start would be Realtor.com, which offers a page to easily search for foreclosed properties at **www.realtor.com/foreclosure**. You can search by state, city, county, neighborhood, and address. Other criteria include home value, size, age of home, number of bedrooms, number of bathrooms, and more.

In addition, many banks and lenders post their REOs on their web sites. The list includes some of the biggest brands in the business, such as Wells Fargo (**https://reo.wellsfargo.com**), CitiMortgage (**https://citimortgage .res.net**), PNC (**www.pnc.com/en/about-pnc/company-profile/pnc-realty -services.html**), and Regions (**www.regions.com/personal_banking/ property_for_sale.rf**).

Plenty of regional banks also list their properties on their web sites. And don't forget about **HomePath.com**, which is operated by Fannie Mae.

BiggerPockets offers a handy list of search sites at **www.biggerpockets .com/rei/bank-owned-reo**.

CASH, CASH, AND CASH

There are two main ways to purchase foreclosed properties: foreclosure auctions and direct purchase from the lender or insuring agency. There are two schools of thought when it comes to the actual transaction. One is using creative techniques while the homeowner is still in pre-foreclosure presenting several options for low out-of-pocket deals. I'll talk about these in the next chapter. The other is in mainstream foreclosure investment where you are buying a house from a lender who has already foreclosed. The bank officers are anxious to get the property off their books, but they are not going to be open to creative financing deals. They want to get money from the property. Cash, cold hard cash, which is due on sale. There will be no extra time to arrange for financing. You need everything lined up at the auction and have a cashier's check in your hand. The real estate auction is no place for "no-money-down" dealers.

$$$ *Part-Time Real Estate Investor Tip* $$$

Depending on the circumstances, you will often be faced with a situation at a foreclosure auction where detailed inspection of the property is not possible. Often an inside inspection is not allowed, the house is locked up, and there isn't even a "for sale" sign. The only pre-bid inspection you can do is to walk around the perimeter and peek in the windows. Properties at auction are usually sold "as is" with none of the usual disclosures. As such, you have to take your best guess based on the information you have.

It will be virtually impossible to find a lender who will simply allow you to "take over payments." Non-qualifying assumable loans are not being written any more, and there are very few in existence. If you're lucky, you may find one every now and then, but don't count on it for the basis of your business. You will need either the cash or the good credit to qualify for a new loan.

If you do have excellent credit, however, the lender holding the REO may be willing to write you a new loan and may be willing to offer you special incentives not usually available. Always ask and don't take what they offer at face value. You may be able to talk them into giving you a loan at a more attractive interest rate or with no points. Also, ask the lender to assume all closing costs. They won't always do this, but always ask because they are often willing to deal.

HOW MUCH TO BID?

The lender who owns the property wants to get as much as possible out of it while still selling it as quickly as possible; and you, the investor, want to buy the property for as little as possible. Somewhere in the middle is a good deal for everyone. The first thing to do is to get a fairly good idea of what the property is actually worth. This may be difficult, because a thorough inspection may not be allowed (especially in the case of auction), but get as good a look at the house as you can, and then research the neighborhood to find out what comparable homes in the same area are selling for. To make it profitable for you, you should be able to buy the foreclosure for 20 percent lower than the full market rate.

There is a reason for not going too far below that figure. Suppose you find a foreclosed home that you estimate could reasonably be valued at $100,000. Bidding $90,000 would probably win you the property, and you'd get a $10,000 profit. Now 10 grand sounds pretty good, but one thing to keep in mind is that there are always going to be some unexpected expenses. You may be paying interest on your loan for longer than you expect if the market goes soft; there may be unexpected repairs that you didn't see, and you may have to spend money to get squatters off the property.

CHAPTER 11

Playing the Good Guy

Nobody wants to be the bad guy. Even real estate investors don't like to be the guy who shows up at someone's door with an eviction notice. The bad news: Sometimes you do have to be the bad guy. The good news: Sometimes you can be a hero. Make no mistake; you're in the real estate business to make money. If your primary motivation in life is being a good guy, then go down and volunteer to hand out food at the homeless shelter. As a real estate investor, buyer, seller, and landlord, though, sometimes you have to be the "heavy." You're "the man." You're the one your tenants hide from when they don't have the money to pay. And no matter how nice you try to be, sometimes people will curse you behind your back. Even though you probably are a pretty nice guy at the end of the day, you have to develop a thick skin to be in this business.

But when you have something that other people want, and you can figure out a way to let them have it, you're the good guy. When you have a way to solve somebody else's problems, then you're also the good guy. In this chapter, I'm going to talk about how to make money by being the good guy.

THE FORECLOSURE SCENARIO

People do get into financial trouble from time to time. They may fall behind on their mortgage payments, and their lender may be threatening foreclosure. What is going through these people's minds when this occurs? It's a terrifying prospect. They are experiencing fear, anger, and dread all at once. They don't know what to do or where they are going to go. They are desperate for a solution but see none. Sometimes they may be in denial and may ignore the problem until the sheriff shows up at their door to remove them physically from the property. If a lender has threatened foreclosure, usually the homeowner has very few options. They don't have the money to get current and probably are not creditworthy enough to borrow it. They are under time pressure, so they probably don't have enough time to sell the house, and even if they did, often there's not enough equity in it to make the deal happen.

The homeowner may have worked many years to establish good credit, and now that good credit is in jeopardy. A foreclosure destroys credit. Once it happens, the homeowner will still owe the arrears and more. It could take years for them to recover.

HERE COMES THE MAN IN THE TALL WHITE HAT

With nowhere to turn and disaster looming on the horizon, you come into the picture and solve all their problems—and make some profit for yourself in the process. Don't make the mistake of thinking this technique is foolproof, though. Not all of the techniques in this book or in any other book are foolproof, regardless of what the advertisement may say. Every deal will require a different approach. Nothing works the same way every time in real estate.

When you appear on the scene and approach the homeowners in distress, they may be willing to talk to you, they may welcome you, or they may not let you in the door. You just have to try it out. If you try enough of these deals, a certain percentage of them will work out well for you.

PRE-FORECLOSURE

You'll hear a lot about "pre-foreclosure" in the real estate business, but in reality this term means nothing. "Foreclosure" is a legal term with a specific meaning; that is, a lender is taking back somebody's house for non-payment. But pre-foreclosure is a fuzzier term. A homeowner can be said to be in pre-foreclosure anywhere between the time they are a day late with a payment up until the time the bank files formal foreclosure papers with the court. When a homeowner is in pre-foreclosure, they can make the problem go away just by throwing money at it. It is the state of pre-foreclosure that causes the most anxiety, because the homeowner does not know what will happen. They have a problem that they are having a hard time fixing, and they know that if they don't fix it they will lose their home.

$$$ *Part-Time Real Estate Investor Tip* $$$

The good news for the homeowner is that, until their home gets sold at auction, they still retain some element of control while they are in a state of "pre-foreclosure." For you, the investor, this also presents an opportunity. It will almost always be easier to make a deal with an individual in pre-foreclosure, rather than make a deal with a bank.

Finding the deals

Finding properties that have already been foreclosed upon is usually a lot easier, but finding the ones that are in the process takes a little more work. Of course, you want to scour the internet. A good place to start is at RealtyTrac, which offers a wealth of resources including a web page that allows you to search for pre-foreclosure opportunities in every state: **www .realtytrac.com/mapsearch/pre-foreclosures**. You might also want to check **www.preforeclosure.com,** which also allows for a robust search of pre-foreclosure opportunities.

Another place to check is your local newspaper, the online and paper classifieds. Check the legal ads in the local daily, or if your community has a business newspaper of some sort, check that. You will be able to find the names and addresses of individuals who are in pre-foreclosure and then approach them to try to make a deal.

How you approach them is up to you; some people find it works well simply to walk up to the door unannounced and say you'd like to buy their house. The downside to that is you are very likely to encounter some cranky people. Others use a more indirect approach of creating a well-worded letter and mailing it to the homeowner and then following up with a phone call. Some investors have had success with advertising. Place a simple newspaper ad that reads something like, "Foreclosure looming? I can help. Call xxx-xxxx."

Be sympathetic. The homeowners want to talk to people who understand their situation and are not going to pass judgment on their failure. Tell them you may be able to help them out and would be interested in making a deal with them to buy the house and get them out of foreclosure.

Chances are they may have already talked to real estate agents who want to list the house, but they probably don't see that as a good solution. They are desperate for a way out and don't want to wait around for the house to sell. Even if the agent has buyers lined up, the agent's commission may be a deal-breaker if the homeowners have very little equity in the home. They could wind up having to pay either way. And that's the last thing they want to do. Nobody wants to pay for the privilege of losing their home.

Your solution, pure and simple, is that you will make their debt go away, protect their credit from getting any worse than it already is, and allow them to get out of their situation gracefully and without having to pay any more money.

$$$ *Part-Time Real Estate Investor Tip* $$$

Pre-foreclosure is not a "no-money-down" proposition. If you're playing the "good guy" and acquiring properties by getting people out of financial trouble, you need cash in your pocket. Without a bankroll at your disposal, nobody will see you as the "good guy." A problem exists, and money—your money—can solve that problem. End of story.

What the homeowner wants from you

The most important part of this strategy is to understand precisely what the homeowner wants. To make the deal work and to convince them to let you take over the house, you have to satisfy the homeowner's needs. Of course, they want to get out of trouble, but there are other demands that could make or break your deal. They may want, and you may be in a position to offer, any number of things, including:

Some cash for equity. Depending on the deal, you may be able to offer them cash for some part of their equity and still make a good profit.

Moving money. Even if they have no equity to speak of, the homeowner may be in desperate straits and have no money with which to move. Offering them $1,000 or $2,000 in cash would solve their problem very quickly, and allow them to vacate the house sooner — which is good for you, too.

Time. The homeowner may be willing to make a deal with you but asks for 30 days or 60 days before they have to move. If this is the case, proceed with caution, because they could delay things far beyond their promised move date. Make your deal and sign the papers with the expected move date in writing. Make sure that any money you plan to give the home-owner as part of the deal does not change hands until they have actually vacated the property.

Stay and rent. This is often a workable situation, where you actually buy the property and then rent it to the former owners. You get immediate tenants. They are relieved of their former burden and still get to stay in their home.

Variations on the "good guy" deal

There are dozens of ways to make this work. Here are a few:

Equity situation. When homeowners are in pre-foreclosure and have a significant amount of equity in the home, they stand to lose all that equity if foreclosure takes place. In such a situation, you may need to make a closer deal with the homeowner that may mean you either (a) writing them a check in addition to taking over their loan, or (b) cutting them in on the profits of your deal once you sell.

"Subject to." This is a creative way of acquiring a house. In this case, you use your cash to make all the homeowner's back payments and catch their mortgage up to date. But instead of taking out a new loan right away, you execute a contract between you and the homeowner in distress that allows you to purchase the property subject to the original loan. From that point on, you make the timely monthly payments instead of the original home-owner. Read more about this in Chapter 18.

Short sale. In this sort of arrangement, instead of dealing with the home-owners, you deal directly with the lender, offering to buy the home at a discount quickly, saving them the trouble of foreclosing and selling the property at auction. This method only works if the homeowner has already received a notice of default and you have a large amount of cash or the ability to qualify for a new loan.

Conventional loan. Of course, the by-the-book way of doing it always works, because it simply involves using your own cash or getting a new loan to purchase the property outright.

Buying a house with multiple existing liens

A homeowner in distress may find themselves with several existing liens against the property. In addition to the primary mortgage, there may be a second mortgage, contractor's liens, tax liens, or any number of other judgments. It may even happen that the total amount of all the liens against the property exceeds the property's value. This isn't a hopeless situation. You may still be able to make a deal and walk away with a good profit.

Here's why you can make a deal: If the house goes to foreclosure and gets sold at auction, then all claims outside of the primary underlying mortgage will very likely get wiped out and holders of those liens will get nothing. As a result, they will be quite willing to work with you and accept a deep discount on the amount due rather than take a chance on suing a bankrupt homeowner or getting claims wiped out by an auction sale. Most creditors will agree that it's better to settle for half rather than wait for the foreclosure and probably get nothing. (Tax liens will survive however, so make sure to get all the details on past due taxes.)

The "good guy" strategy of acquiring property can be challenging. The main element of this strategy is the ability to find solutions to problems and to be able to negotiate with multiple parties. You are a problem-solver. But don't forget: You are not just solving the homeowner's problems; you may also be solving the lender's problems and the problems of multiple lien-holders as well.

CHAPTER 12

The Fixer-Upper Opportunity

First impressions are very powerful. Imagine walking into a house for sale. It's been sitting empty for more than a year, and it's selling at substantially below the market rate. Outside, the yard has not been mowed and is overgrown. When you walk in, the electricity and water have been shut off. It's dusty, one of the rooms smells like cats, and the kitchen has old, crusty linoleum on the floor. You notice a crack in the wall in the living room, and the carpet is an ugly shade of purple. The bathroom sink is cracked, the drain pipe is hanging askew and probably leaks, and the shower door is broken. The basement is full of old clothes and empty cardboard boxes. "Ugh, this place is nasty," you say. "I'm getting out of here."

The proper response would be, "Ugh, this place is nasty. I'm going to make an offer."

Small, cosmetic things can turn off a buyer immediately, but as an investor, you have to look beyond those things. Presumably, you have a lawnmower. You can cut the grass in a few hours or hire a neighborhood kid to do it for ten bucks. Dust and smell can be cleaned in an afternoon with a mop, bucket, and some Mr. Clean. Linoleum can be replaced, plaster can be patched, and carpet can be ripped out. A new bathroom sink and a shower door can be purchased for about a hundred dollars each, and installed single-handedly in a day. Basement clutter can be cleaned out. You can do it all yourself or hire a handyman to come in and help you for a couple days. For a few thousand dollars, you could transform that ugly house into the pride of the block—and then jack up the price accordingly.

The fact is, many fixer-uppers are actually good houses that have just fallen into disrepair. In most cases, repairs are just several small things that need attention. The cumulative effect of all those small things is to create the impression of a poor house, but that is just "first impression." When looking at a fixer, keep an eye toward what really needs to be fixed and how easy it would be to do it. Look beyond that first impression, and imagine what it would look like after you and your clean-up crew had a week to work on it. That's not to say you won't come across money pits—houses that have so much to be done that it's not worth it at any price—but that's why you do your pre-purchase inspection, so you know ahead of time what you are getting yourself into.

$$$ *Part-Time Real Estate Investor Tip* $$$

etting the price. Taking the original cost of the house, adding on acquisition costs and repair costs, and then factoring in a percentage for profit to arrive at a final sales price will not work well. Work backwards instead. Determine what a home in good shape would go for in the neighborhood you are in and set your price accordingly. Subtract your profit margin of, say, 20 percent. Then subtract what you estimate you will need for repairs, and then you will have an idea of a maximum figure you should pay for the property. For example: You estimate your renovated house will sell for $100,000. You don't want to put any more than $80,000 into it. Renovation costs will be $10,000. Therefore, your cost of acquisition (purchase price, closing costs, interest while you are doing repairs) should be no more than $70,000. Don't forget to factor in interest expense, keeping in mind that you may have to carry a mortgage for several months while you renovate and then list the house for sale.

Novice real estate investors and even some seasoned ones often make a big mistake when they evaluate a property for purchase. That is, they mistake the pre-purchase inspection for a checklist of things that the seller must fix before they are willing to make a deal. This approach severely limits you as an investor, and at the end of the day, limits the amount of profits you can take out of a property. Sometimes, the worst house in a neighborhood will be more profitable to you than the prettiest one.

WHAT IS A FIXER-UPPER?

Simply put, it's a house that needs work. The understanding is that the buyer is going to take it "as is" and do the work himself (or contract it out). Many investors make a very successful business of buying fixers, renovating them, and then either selling them at a profit or renting them out.

The advantage is that you are able to buy the house a lot cheaper than you would otherwise, and that means you can buy more properties with the same amount of resources. When you go into the business of fixer-uppers, the pre-purchase inspection (see Chapter 26) becomes very important, but the purpose of this inspection is quite different. People buying a home for themselves to live in often use this inspection as a way to weed out bad properties and to make sure there are no flaws in a property. They use it as a negotiating tool and as a way to get the seller to make necessary repairs as part of the sales contract.

But buying fixers for investment is different. You do want to be aware of all existing flaws and necessary repairs ahead of time, but the purpose of having this information isn't to force the seller to make those repairs. Instead, you want to be advised ahead of time on the needed repairs, so you can get a good idea of how much time and money you will have to spend on them.

$$$ *Part-Time Real Estate Investor Tip* $$$

The best real estate investment isn't necessarily going to be the one that looks pretty. You know all the tricks real estate people use when showing a house: slap on a little paint, put some cookies in the oven, and plant a few flowers by the door. In reality, these things are meaningless. They are just sales techniques, and you must look beyond these superficial frills. You'll use them yourself later on. What you want to find is a house that isn't in good shape, that hasn't been maintained, and probably has some dirt on the floor. A house in cosmetic disarray will sell for less, but these cosmetic things are easy to fix. As long as the house is structurally sound, things like cracks in the wall, faded paint, leaky pipes, dirt, and clutter can be fixed quickly and cheaply—and after you have fixed them, you will add thousands of dollars of value to the house.

AN UGLY HOUSE IN A GOOD NEIGHBORHOOD OR AN UGLY HOUSE IN AN UGLY NEIGHBORHOOD

Okay, you just bought an ugly house. That's okay. A fixer-upper is supposed to be ugly, at least until you've had a chance to work on it for a while, but the neighborhood will be a big factor in how much you can re-sell or rent the house for.

Suppose your fixer is in an upper class neighborhood. You bought the ugliest house on the block. You have a good chance of fixing it up and selling it for a big profit. In such a case, you may want to adjust the nature of your renovations to match the other houses in the block. If every house on the block has excellent landscaping, put some money into landscaping. If they all have swimming pools or hot tubs, put in a swimming pool or a hot tub. In an upscale neighborhood, these sorts of additions may bring a higher price and may even be necessary to compete.

But in a marginal neighborhood, the type of repairs and renovations you make will be quite different. Putting a sunken swimming pool in the back yard of a home in a blighted neighborhood won't be a good idea, and it won't increase the home's value significantly. Focus more on functional renovations.

That said, you can make a profit in both a good and a bad neighborhood. Besides fixing houses, you can also fix entire neighborhoods. In a blighted neighborhood, you may find that multiple houses in the same block are available for purchase at low prices, and you can wind up owning nearly an entire block. This gives you tremendous control. Work with neighborhood associations and city planners toward renovating an entire neighborhood, and you'll not only make a tidy profit, you'll also be seen as a community hero.

FIXER-UPPERS ARE EASY TO BUY WITH BAD CREDIT

Some lenders don't like to deal with financing fixers. Coupled with the fact that they are desirable only to a small number of people (like you and me) and they have probably been sitting empty for months or even years, sellers tend to be very flexible on terms. The more repair and renovation that needs to be done, the easier it will be to buy on creative terms.

Find a fixer that needs some serious cosmetic repair that has been sitting empty for a long time, and make a creative offer. You have a good chance of having it accepted. The seller may be willing to sell it to you on land contract terms, or perhaps carry a substantial second mortgage (which would help you more easily secure a first from a conventional lender). You may even be able to get it on lease option terms, or if you are paying cash, with a substantial discount. The fact is, if it has been sitting empty for more than a year, the seller may have already given up hope of ever selling it, and anything you offer will be better than nothing.

Here's a creative concept for buying a fixer that needs a lot of work: Offer to buy it on a land contract or a "subject to" contract, but with graduated terms: While you are making renovations, your payments will be reduced by half. After renovations are completed, you start making full payments and then make up the difference when you are able to resell the house.

FIXER-UPPERS GIVE YOU MORE NEGOTIATING POWER

Again, because the seller has very few potential customers, you are in the driver's seat when it comes to buying a fixer-upper. The longer it has been sitting empty and the uglier it is, the more you can negotiate, not just on the purchase terms but also on the price.

After you have inspected the property, you will have made a list of repairs that you plan to do. Create a bill of materials to show how much you will have to spend to bring the property up to par. It doesn't have to be precise or exact; it's just to provide a general idea of how much money you will spend after you make the deal. When you negotiate price, have this bill of materials in hand. Suppose your total materials cost will be $10,000 and the seller wants $100,000 for the house. Offer no more than $90,000, and produce your bill of materials as support for your offer.

DOING THE FIXING

There are different levels of fixing up that you could do. If you're planning to live in the house yourself, then the sky's the limit. But if you're going to try to turn a profit, you have to restrict yourself. You don't need to install the $1,000 marble countertop when a hundred-dollar synthetic one will do nicely.

Also, approach contractors with caution. Building contractors want to suck all the profit out of the fixer before you have a chance to, so use them sparingly and only when absolutely necessary. Keep in mind that union shops in particular, while politically correct, will make steep demands on your pocketbook.

$$$ *Part-Time Real Estate Investor Tip* $$$

One thing I've learned over the years is that home repairs are not rocket science. Many people are intimidated by the thought of installing a sink or putting in some tile, and if you are intimidated by these things, fixer-uppers are not for you. High-priced contractors like to create the image of a virtual priesthood of specialized knowledge. Of course, they are usually good at what they do, but they didn't have to get a Ph.D. to learn it. They may have taken a trade course or two or just picked it up as they went along. You can do many of the repairs yourself if you are generally handy, even if you have not done it before, just by reading a brochure, checking the internet, and asking the guy at the home supply store a few questions.

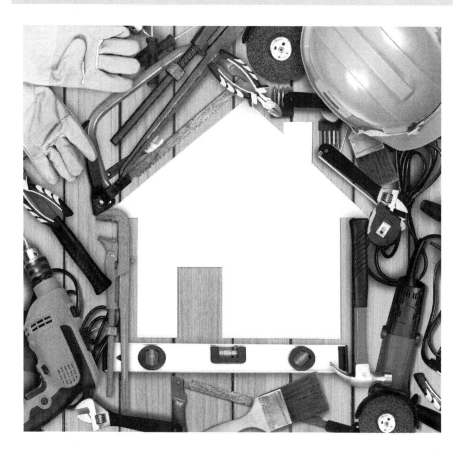

CHAPTER 13

HUD Homes

HUD homes (**www.hudhomestore.com/Home/Index.aspx**) represent an excellent opportunity for future homeowners or for investors. However, the rules are a bit different. Before you embark on a search for a HUD home deal, you must first understand a bit about this government agency, its history, and its mission.

The Federal Housing Administration (FHA), which is part of Housing and Urban Development (HUD), was created by the federal government to promote a particular social goal: more homeownership in America. Its primary mission, then, is not to create more landlords and investors. Its primary mission is to put more people in homes that they own. But that doesn't rule out your participation as an investor and speculator.

The FHA is a self-funded organization; it costs taxpayers nothing. It depends on the revenues that it generates, not tax money. As a result, social goals notwithstanding, it does present opportunities to investors. Any organization dealing with mortgages will have a certain percent of defaults, and HUD's default rate is higher than most, since they deal primarily with first-time buyers who may be in lower income categories and have other challenges. The result is a brisk secondary market for foreclosed homes.

WHAT HUD DOES

Simply put, HUD has created a system that allows more people to buy and inhabit their own homes than would otherwise be possible if HUD did not exist. FHA was created in the 1930s during the Great Depression as a way of stabilizing the sinking housing and mortgage markets. The agency has a number of different programs that target first-time buyers, minorities, those with less than perfect credit, and those who wish to move into neighborhoods undergoing urban renewal. For the most part, HUD deals in single-family homes that are under a given dollar amount (which varies by state). As such, HUD homes are not usually high-end luxury homes, but rather, basic "bread and butter" homes for working people.

HUD does not make loans directly to people; rather, they guarantee loans that are made by conventional lenders. They charge a fee for this guarantee in the form of mortgage insurance premiums, which are paid by the homeowner.

When a homeowner falls behind on payments, the lender can foreclose. But instead of the lender taking back the property directly and trying to re-sell it, HUD will pay the lender the amount of their losses and take the property themselves. Here is where the opportunity lies. Because HUD is a very large agency that guarantees millions of mortgages, there are naturally going to be a large number of foreclosed homes in their portfolio. FHA insured mortgages make up nearly a third of all insured mortgages in the country. At any given time, about one out of nine FHA mortgages is in a delinquent state, although FHA does allow the homeowner several opportunities to avoid foreclosure through special forbearance programs and other workout deals. And since HUD's mission is not to be landlords, they don't want to hold on to these properties; instead, they put them up for sale to the general public. They give first priority to homeowners who want to buy the foreclosed homes, but when they don't sell, HUD gives investors a chance to bid.

WYSIWYG (WHAT YOU SEE IS WHAT YOU GET)

When you bid on a HUD home, you're getting it "as is." HUD will not make improvements to the property. That's up to you as the buyer/investor.

By all means, you should do your own pre-purchase inspection before making a bid. You may not make a bid that is subject to inspection or other conditions or contingencies, however; and that's why you need to know ahead of time as much as you possibly can about the property.

HUD does recommend that you have a professional inspection done prior to making your bid, but there is a downside to that. If you are an investor that is "fishing" for properties, having a professional inspection done on multiple properties gets to be quite expensive, and so it is better for investors who want to specialize in HUD REO properties to become adept at doing their own inspections.

If HUD is aware of a particular defect or problem with a property, they will disclose that information. Don't take this disclosure to mean that HUD has a policy of "full disclosure." It just means that if they know about a flaw, they will tell you about it. It's up to you to determine the condition of the property and what needs to be fixed.

RED TAPE AND BUREAUCRACY

Have you ever dealt with a government agency? Government agencies and bureaucracies tend to be inflexible, and they tend to have their own set of rules. Bidding on a HUD property is not like making a bid on another piece of property. Normally, for example, offers can be written using any type of valid generic form, but when you are bidding on a HUD home, HUD requires a very specific set of paperwork. You can only use HUD-approved forms. Any bid that arrives that does not comply precisely with their guidelines and instructions will be refused. Don't count on HUD to call you up and tell you that you used the wrong form. Instead, you'll just get it back in the mail, and you may miss the deadline as a result.

$$$ *Part-Time Real Estate Investor Tip* $$$

HUD is well known for offering low-down mortgages, but these are available to homeowners, not to investors. HUD does not offer financing to investors. You'll need to have either the cash available or be able to get outside financing.

There will be an initial "priority period" during which each home will be offered only to homeowners. Most of the properties listed by HUD are available only to homeowners. You will be able to tell which ones are available to investors right on the list that is available at no charge on the HUD website at **www.hudhomestore.com/Home/Index.aspx**. Following that priority period, if the home has not sold, HUD opens the bidding up to all buyers.

During the second phase, or "regular bid" process, a date is set, and all bids must be in by that date. Then the bids are opened and the highest acceptable offer is accepted. But what if no acceptable offers came in during that time? HUD still has the home, and you have a chance to bid again. The property is put on the "extended" list, and during this time, there is no deadline—instead, HUD just opens up all offers every day—and will take the first acceptable offer.

Should you buy a home off of the "extended" list? Absolutely. Remember, though, these are the ones nobody else wants. By the time they have made the "extended" list, it has already been determined that there are no owner-occupants that want the home. HUD has set a "full price" level and opened it for bidding, and nobody wanted to pay the full price. It's anybody's guess at this point what HUD will accept, and this extended period is where you will find the best deals. Keep in mind that homes that are on the "extended" list are probably serious fixer-uppers, but don't let that scare you off. Those are the ones you want, because they will deliver you the greatest profit after you renovate them.

Some real estate brokers are under contract with HUD and they list the HUD properties locally; and if you prefer, you can use this real estate broker to submit your offer on your behalf. Usually HUD will pay the real estate broker's commissions and most other closing costs, but make sure this is specifically written out in your offer. The real estate agent gets a customary 6 percent commission. The agent will be able to assist you in the bid process and the convoluted HUD paperwork.

HUD evaluates based on their net proceeds. That means, you can make an offer where HUD pays all the closing costs and real estate commissions, but another offer will win because that buyer will pay half the closing costs.

$$$ Part-Time Real Estate Investor Tip $$$

HUD homes are sold by sealed bid. This means you don't have any idea what other people may be bidding. HUD does list a "full price" for each property, and if a full price offer comes in, it will be taken immediately. If no full price offers are made, it is open for bidding. The trick here is to try to second-guess what other people will do. Chances are, if bidding has already been opened up to investors, nobody will bid full price. It's up to you to gauge how much interest you think there will be, determine how much profit you think you can make, and make your bid accordingly.

When determining your bid, take a look at other HUD properties in the same area that have sold and calculate the difference between the full price and the selling price. For example, if a home had been listed by HUD for $100,000, but it sold for $90,000, that means HUD accepted a bid for 90 percent of the asking price, and you would therefore have a fairly good chance of using that ratio as a basis for your other bids.

A GOOD SOURCE OF "FIXER" PROPERTY DEALS

Homeowners get first crack at HUD foreclosures, but this doesn't mean that investors are left with nothing. The homes that are in desirable neighborhoods and in perfect condition are more likely to go to people who are going to buy them to live in. Investors should see HUD instead as a source of fixer-upper investments that can be turned around and resold for a profit after renovation. Homeowners are less likely to buy the properties that need a lot of cosmetic repair. But you as a real estate investor will understand that an ugly house can be made beautiful, often without a large investment. And it's the ugly HUD homes that homeowners don't want to bother with that will be the best investments for you.

One thing to look out for is that although the majority of HUD properties are single-family houses, HUD also occasionally has other properties, such as duplexes or triplexes, vacant lands, or condominiums for sale.

During a "down" economy and period of high unemployment, the number of HUD foreclosures goes up dramatically, especially since homeowners taking advantage of FHA guarantees are marginal to begin with, and many would not be able to get a home at all were it not for the FHA program. These people are not wealthy and are most vulnerable to slow economic times — and are more prone to losing their homes than other homeowners. What this means for you as an investor is that a recession is a particularly good opportunity to acquire homes. Not everybody suffers from a recession, and real estate investors in particular can use recessionary economies to their advantage. *Don't take a recessionary economy as an excuse not to make money!* Too often, would-be investors and entrepreneurs don't take action, thinking, "Oh, the economy is too bad right now. I'm not going to invest." That's the wrong approach. An investor and entrepreneur must always be on the lookout for opportunities, regardless of macroeconomic conditions. And they must be attuned to which opportunities work best in which economies.

If you are a homeowner who wants to buy a home to live in, FHA has great deals for you and several programs available that will get you into a home with a very small down payment. But these deals are not going to be available to you as an investor. HUD foreclosures are not "no-money-down" deals—you're on your own to come up with the financing or the cash.

When recessions hit, as they inevitably will, the number of HUD foreclosures skyrockets. This means two things for you: (1) there are more properties to choose from, and (2) HUD is likely to offer special deals, quicker closings, and possibly even financing to the right investor.

CHAPTER 14

Tax Sales

In the last chapter, we looked at the fact that occasionally people fall behind on their mortgage payments, and their homes get foreclosed upon. These foreclosed homes then present a buying opportunity for you, the investor. But buying foreclosures is not the only way to profit from repossessed homes. Who else repossesses homes? Yes, that's right—Uncle Sam.

Even if a home is completely paid off, there are still property taxes, and if they don't get paid, the government is usually pretty quick to respond. If you don't pay those taxes, your home could wind up being owned by your county government. Many homes that are taken by county governments in lieu of taxes due are homes that have been abandoned. There are, to be sure, cases where somebody's grandmother who has lived in a house for 60 years can't pay their taxes and, tragically, loses the old family home. But most cases aren't quite so sympathetic. Right here in my own hometown, local property taxes have risen over the past couple years, and landlords who own homes in marginal areas find their properties suddenly unprofitable and abandon them. An abandoned house with an existing mortgage may get repossessed by the lender, but if the conditions are right, it may be acquired by the municipality for back taxes.

I can't imagine a landlord completely abandoning a house, even if taxes have gone up. Renovations can be done, the property improved, and value added to it. There's always a way to derive value from a piece of property without walking away from it. Abandonment is almost always a poor strategy; yet many people do it. In most cases, those who abandoned the property could have made it work for them with the right strategy. Those who do abandon properties like that are often slumlords who do virtually no maintenance or renovation on properties. They take the easy profits off the surface, but don't take that extra step to derive the greater profits by improving the property.

Their poor choice is your opportunity.

A TAX LIEN CERTIFICATE

Usually, when you buy properties for back taxes, you are actually buying a tax lien certificate, and you acquire the property some time down the road. It's a time-consuming process, but it can be very profitable. Here's how the tax lien certificate works. When homeowners get behind on their taxes, the county government will place a lien on their property. Depending on the municipality, there is a period of time during which the homeowner can pay the back taxes and have the lien removed, but after a certain period of time, the government will sell those tax liens at auction to investors.

As an investor, you attend an auction and bid on the tax liens, not the property itself. If you win the bidding, you then own the lien against the property. This way, the county government can get their money from the property from you, the investor, when the property owner cannot pay. But that doesn't mean you can move in right away. The owners still have some rights. They will have a period of time after you purchase the lien to clear the tax debt. But the catch is that after you have made your investment, the homeowner then must also pay you interest in addition to the amount of money you paid for the lien to get their home back. The interest is usually substantial, often between 18 and 24 percent per annum, and is set by the county government. In a few cases, the interest is not pro-rated, and the homeowner must pay the entire 24 percent (or whatever percent is statutory), even if they pay off the debt within a month or two. If the owners pay you back your investment plus interest, they get the home back.

If they do not perform during the predetermined period of time set by the county, you become owner of the real estate.

Either way, you win. Either you get a high rate of interest on your money or you get the real estate. Note, too, that when title of the property does eventually fall to you, you receive it free and clear of any junior liens.

$$$ *Part-Time Real Estate Investor Tip* $$$

Taxes always take priority and get paid before anything else when there is a foreclosure making buying tax liens a solid investment — since you don't have to worry about somebody with another lien coming in and wiping out your claim. If you own the tax lien, you have the superior claim in every case.

A major advantage to this technique as an income strategy is that even when you do not acquire the property, you are gaining revenue. Those who put money into certificates of deposit, bonds, or stocks usually won't get the same high rate of return. A deposit certificate may yield you 2 percent these days. If you play the stock market shrewdly, maybe you would get 10 percent, or maybe 15 percent on a decent year. But then again, the stock market can take a turn for the worse and you can lose. Stocks are far from a sure bet, no matter how much you study the market—you never really know for sure whether you will end the year ahead or behind. When you put your money into tax liens, however, you'll always end the year in the black.

When you buy the tax lien, you're not buying the property—not right away, anyway. You are simply buying the county's accounts receivable on the taxes. That means the owners have to pay you, instead of the county, for the back taxes (and interest).

After the waiting period, having given the homeowner the statutory amount of time to pay their tax debt and interest, you get to be in the driver's seat. If the owner does not pay you back the amount of money you paid for the lien plus a high rate of interest, you may foreclose on the property, obtain title to it, and evict the residents. You then own the property and may do with it as you will.

THE PROCESS

How do you go about buying tax liens? Unfortunately, it's different in every county. The good news is that in many states, people can buy tax lien certificates via the internet. However, every county has a different policy regarding such auctions. Some will partner with a third-party firm to conduct online auctions. Others prefer more traditional auctions. To check if a particular county sells tax lien certificates online, you'll have to do some legwork. You can usually find all the information you need just by making a few phone calls to your county office.

Most publish a list of properties and then hold auctions periodically. The county may require you to post a bond to attend or show proof of ability to pay. Each lien that comes up for auction will have a minimum bid and sometimes it may be very low, even less than $1,000.

And yes, it happens—and happens often. Investors buy tax liens for only a few thousand dollars and then are able to foreclose on the home later on and acquire title to the property. In many cases, this is the absolute cheapest way to buy property, usually much cheaper than buying foreclosures. The downside is the waiting period.

Most states use this tax lien process, but there are some which instead sell tax deeds, which are not always a good deal. Tax liens are always a good bet, but those few states that don't use tax liens will sell properties for market value or for the total amount of judgments against the property, including mortgages. Naturally, it's better to obtain a tax lien and then foreclose on the property yourself and wipe out all inferior claims!

Whenever possible, inspect the property as thoroughly as you can. As I discussed above, many of these properties have been abandoned by unscrupulous slumlords who do not maintain their rental properties. But, as with foreclosures, you shouldn't be scared away by the prospect of having to do repairs. Instead, the fact that a property needs some repairs is a tremendous opportunity for you to increase your profits. And as with foreclosures, your ability to inspect the property may vary from county to county. There may be people still living in the property, and while you can certainly knock on the door and ask them to show it to you, they are under no obligation to do so and may even become hostile. If the house is vacant, the county may have a procedure for inspecting the property, but you will likely be limited to just a cursory inspection. Even if you are able to bring in your own inspectors, it usually doesn't make sense to do so, since the cost of the inspections must be paid by you whether you win the auction or not. Like many foreclosures, you look at the property, sometimes only from the outside, and make your best guess. Even if there are thousands of dollars' worth of repairs that need to be made, remember that you're still getting the property at a bargain.

YOU WIN EITHER WAY

When you buy the lien, you either (a) eventually acquire the property, or (b) the homeowner pays their obligation and you earn a very high rate of interest. Either way, you can't lose. How much interest do you get when you buy a CD at the bank? As of the middle of 2016, rates were well below 1 percent, even for longer-term CDs. The interest you are entitled to on the tax lien is much higher, often between 5 percent and 36 percent, as set by law. This interest is paid typically over six months to three years.

If you do end up with the property, what type of property can you get? You never know what's going to come up for auction. Most of them will be older properties that need some work, perhaps that have been abandoned and vacant for years. If that's the case, you can do some renovation and turn it into an income-producing property. Once in a while, you'll find a gem. There are true anecdotes of investors who purchased properties at tax auctions for a few thousand dollars that turned out to be worth over

$100,000. For the most part though, you're not going to see the expensive, suburban homes going up for tax auction. These will be fixer-upper properties that you will need to do some work on.

$$$ *Part-Time Real Estate Investor Tip* $$$

Finding properties for which you can acquire the tax lien takes a little detective work, but you can usually find out about the process, get a list, and get the auction dates from your county office. The county may charge a small fee for the list, but it is minimal. You will find lots of private companies that offer lists as well, but be aware that you can get the same information yourself. However, if you are looking to acquire multiple tax liens across several geographic regions, buying a list may indeed be a useful strategy to help save you time.

WHY DO COUNTY GOVERNMENTS DO THIS?

One wonders why county governments involve middlemen in the deal and create such a lucrative opportunity for private investors when they could collect the interest themselves. It's simply a matter of cash flow for most counties, which almost always are underfunded and in need of resources. Counties depend on property tax revenue to offer necessary services. They need the money immediately when it is due, because it is figured into their budget. And so, they auction off the liens instead of keeping the liens themselves. That way they are able to get the money immediately and continue funding their services.

Another reason that counties auction off properties for back taxes is urban redevelopment. From a community perspective, it's not in the county's best interest to hold title to a lot of vacant houses. It's better to do anything that is possible and legal to get those properties back on the tax rolls and occupied.

CHAPTER 15

Blighted Areas and Vacant Properties

As an investor in real estate, you have to learn to know what opportunities are in what types of neighborhoods.

Upscale, wealthy neighborhoods along the coast are wonderful to look at, and if you're rich enough to live there, more power to you. But there's not much of a rental market for neighborhoods like that. It's strictly a buy-and-sell marketplace. Who wants to rent a million-dollar home? Not very many people. If you can afford to rent one of those upscale places, you can probably afford to buy something. And when those houses do go on the market, they don't always move quickly.

And the fact is these sorts of neighborhoods, while the house prices have been known to skyrocket, are also the most volatile. There are cities in California, for example, where the price of homes can massively soar when the market is hot. But during real estate crashes — such as the one in 2008 — those same homes could easily lose value significantly.

The best place to invest is somewhere that you can buy a home inexpensively for below market value. Go where the market is "soft" and homes are not selling quickly, and you'll get deals. Find the homes that need work and are in blighted neighborhoods, do the work that needs to be done, and you can reap greater rewards. It's not unusual for investors to deal exclusively in neighborhoods like that and gain a 100 percent profit on a property just by making the house look like a home again.

Here's one such success story. Although I'd never invest in property in California, that's where this story takes place, in scenic Santa Cruz, along the California coast by the Monterey Bay. My friend spotted a house that had been vacant for some time. It was in terrible disrepair, the yard was overgrown, and there were squatters living in it. The house was home to junkies, transients, and runaways who came in and out and even lit fires inside to stay warm at night. The walls, what was left of them, were covered with gang graffiti. It was an eyesore and a nuisance. But it was a case of finding the worst house in a desirable area. Santa Cruz, where I lived for several years, is one of those highly desirable but extremely overpriced cities, where middle-class people get pushed out—leaving, for the most part, only the poor and the rich. (At the time, I was neither, so I left.) My friend was able to acquire this piece of uninhabitable property for $250,000, which was very cheap for Santa Cruz. After visiting the house with the sheriff a few times, he managed to evict all the squatters and set about his repairs. The fortunate thing about it was that, although it was uninhabitable when he bought it, it was still structurally sound, and he was able to turn it into a wonderfully comfortable family home within a year, doubling its value.

$$$ *Part-Time Real Estate Investor Tip* $$$

If you are dealing in vacant homes in blighted areas, you may encounter squatters living in properties you buy. You must get rid of them right away before undertaking any repairs and keep them out — otherwise all your hard work will be destroyed very quickly. This is one area where you cannot afford to have any sympathy. Do not try to evict them yourself. Sometimes they may have a sense of entitlement to the property as their personal "squat," and they may get violent. Always work with local law enforcement to get the job done. Give your phone number to the neighbors, and you will find that they will usually be more than happy to keep an eye out for you.

A WORD ABOUT SECURITY

Vacant homes in blighted areas can become home to squatters, good places for criminals to conduct drug deals, and a source of wealth for scavengers. Here in South Bend, as well as in towns all across America, the price of scrap metal has been going up, and scavengers who roam the town with old pickup trucks looking for discarded scrap metal are often tempted to go into abandoned homes to see what they can find. Sometimes they rip copper pipes out of the walls, and even strip aluminum siding off of the outside, in an attempt to make a few extra dollars at the scrap yard. They can cause thousands of dollars' worth of damage in the process.

When you first start to work on a house, you must make it well known that you have staked your claim and that the property belongs to you and is no longer vacant. Consider posting "no trespassing" and "under renovation" signs. You may even want to install a security alarm system. Make sure all doors are secured and locked when you are not there. Talk to your local police department. Chances are they will be glad to know that somebody is reclaiming a problem property and may be willing to take special notice of your house on their regular patrols.

MY NEIGHBORHOOD

I live in South Bend, Indiana. It's home to the University of Notre Dame and is located about 90 miles east of Chicago. Real estate here is priced lower than the national average and is generally affordable. It's one of those increasingly rare towns where a working man can still afford to buy a home. The West Side of South Bend has a long history as the oldest part of town. In the early days of the town's history in the 1800s, my part of the West Side, the "Near West Side," was home to the wealthy and elite. Huge Victorian and Queen Anne style homes lined the street, and just a few blocks away from my home are two of the most architecturally spectacular mansions in the entire Midwest: The Oliver mansion and the Studebaker mansion.

But urban trends being what they are, in the '60s and '70s people with money moved to the suburbs. The neighborhood deteriorated and became a center for drugs and crime. Most of those beautiful homes either sat empty or were carved up into apartments that were poorly maintained and rented out cheap. Slumlords took over, and Chapin Street, the main thoroughfare of this neighborhood, became known as a center of prostitution, gambling, and drugs. There was a bar located just a few blocks from my home that was well known for regular shootings. It was a neighborhood that people were afraid to go into even in the daytime. You would go out of your way to avoid it. If you had to go through it, you stayed in your car and locked all the doors.

But after a long period of decay, people took notice of the beautiful, historic homes that could be purchased with very little money. People started to buy and restore them. The city took a hand in the renewal effort. Some of the homes were beyond repair and had to be condemned and torn down. Part of Chapin Street, which had a bad reputation that people couldn't get out of their heads, was renamed Dr. Martin Luther King Jr. Drive. The Studebaker Museum (a great place to see mint-condition old cars) was relocated on Chapin Street in a brand new building. The street was renewed and changed from a four-lane thoroughfare into a two-lane residential street with beautiful landscaping and quaint old-fashioned streetlights on both sides. The bar with the bad reputation was shut down. Today, some of those old homes that sat empty and couldn't even be given away are selling briskly.

My own home has a similar history of decay and renewal. It was built in 1888 by a wealthy local family. It stayed in the family until the 1960s when urban decay started to set in. The house, a stately 12-room Victorian, was carved up into three apartments. I've talked to other people in the neighborhood who remember it during that time. I've heard stories of shootings taking place in the upstairs apartment, people getting into terrible fights, and drug dealing taking place. The house was a well-known nuisance.

But a few years ago, a new owner got caught up in the urban renewal, bought the house for a pittance, and converted it back into a single-family home. Landscaping was added and the house was restored to its former glory. I bought it recently and continued the process.

The neighborhood is improving, but still has problem areas — the house across the street is under renovation, and I often see teenagers going into the back yard and into the garage to try to find tools and equipment to steal, but the important thing is that it's going up instead of going down, and homes here are increasing in value. All throughout the West Side are architectural treasures that can still be found for very little money.

"WE BUY UGLY HOUSES"

There's an advertisement I see around town that reads, "We buy ugly houses." It's a simple proclamation, one that strikes some people as unusual. It's the ugly ones that present the greatest opportunity for the most profit.

Consider focusing on one particular neighborhood as a strategy. You may be able to locate such a neighborhood in your own town. Owning multiple homes in one neighborhood has several advantages: It gives you greater control not only over each individual property but over the neighborhood in general. If you own one home on a block, you may not be able to do much about the general condition of neighborhood blight. But if you own the entire block, you're the King of the Neighborhood and you can change that block's character completely—and, as a result, increase the value of every single home there.

EVALUATING THE PROPERTY

Considering how much to offer on a vacant property in a distressed neighborhood is different than making an offer on an occupied property in good condition in a "good" neighborhood. With a conventional property, it's easy to compare prices of neighboring houses and come up with a reasonably good price. But in the distressed neighborhood, you are really buying an opportunity, not just a property. The property itself in its current state may be worth very little, and yes, you can usually buy them for a small sum. But doing the property comparison method to determine a price doesn't work in this case. That's because in this sort of neighborhood, properties are very mixed. There may be a few houses on the block that are abandoned, in disrepair, and worth practically nothing. Yet there may be others that are being renovated or have already been renovated, which have significantly higher value. So instead of just taking an average, you have to consider several things:

1. The current condition of the house

2. The state of the neighborhood

3. How much you will have to spend to renovate the property

4. What you will be able to sell it for (or rent it for) after you renovate it

Additionally, you will want to factor in some "fuzzier" qualities, such as civic pride. Is there a neighborhood association? If so, get involved in it and meet the people on the board. Find out what is going on in the neighborhood, and you will be able to get a good sense for what direction the neighborhood is headed. You may also be able to get inside information on other projects that are going on in the neighborhood and meet other investors that are doing the same thing as you.

To invest in this type of neighborhood, you have to go beyond just looking at properties as they are. You need the ability to see into the future and predict what the neighborhood will become.

CHAPTER 16

Indirect Real Estate Investments

Call it "the lazy man's way to real estate riches."

There are more ways to invest in real estate besides buying, renovating, selling, or renting out property. Those who have little time on their hands can still reap the benefits of real estate without having to do all the heavy lifting. One way of doing this, as I discussed in Chapter 14, was buying real estate tax liens. The lien buying strategy is a sort of halfway point where investors make money both on simply owning the lien itself (through interest) and acquiring the property itself if the homeowner doesn't pay up. For those who don't want to get involved in actually dealing with the property directly, owning a tax lien is only a partial solution, since on some occasions you will actually end up with the property and will then have to do something with it.

REITS

No matter what you invest in, the issue of liquidity is always an issue. No investor wants to have all of their money tied up in long-term deals. Some of it has to be readily accessible. The drawback to real estate investments in general is the liquidity is always a little questionable. But there's a tradeoff. If you put money into a passbook savings account in the bank, you'll gain nearly nothing in interest. But on the plus side, you can walk into the bank and take out money whenever you need it. It's not quite so easy with real estate. Sure, you can sell property, but it doesn't happen immediately.

Investing money in a real estate investment trust (REIT) solves the liquidity problem. When you put money into a REIT, you are absolved of the property management responsibility and are just an investor. REIT shares are bought and sold freely on the open market, just like shares of stock. You can cash them in when you need money, and you can put more funds into the REIT if you like without having to worry about specific properties. In fact, when you own REIT shares, you probably are not even aware of the specific properties that are involved. The REIT fund is simply a large management fund that is used to buy real estate, provide mortgages, or manage rental properties (or some combination).

There are two approaches to REITs. You can invest in an individual REIT or invest in a mutual fund that invests in REITs, which spreads out the risk even more. The REIT is managed by professionals with experience in real estate investment, and they usually provide an excellent return even in a slow economy. Although the return varies, you can certainly expect to get a higher return, and a steadier flow of returns, than you could in the stock market or by investing in CDs or bonds. The return will be much higher than standard money market rates. In fact, research by Cohen & Steers Capital Management of New York shows that over the past 15 years, actively managed REITs generated an annualized average return of 10.6 percent return.

The risk is low with this type of investment, because the fund is backed by equity in real estate, and unlike some stock market funds, are not as speculative. There is real value behind the shares you purchase.

One advantage to a publicly traded REIT is that because it is traded like any other stock, it is regulated by the SEC, and therefore oversight is involved. Publicly traded REITs must comply with standard SEC regulations and must make regular financial disclosures just like any other publicly traded company. Also, because they are bought and sold on an open exchange, you will be able to find a lot of independent analysis and information about such REITs.

$$$ *Part-Time Real Estate Investor Tip* $$$

You don't have to be a big wheel to invest in REITs. There is no minimum investment required for most publicly traded REITs.

BUYING PRIVATE MORTGAGE CONTRACTS

There is a vibrant secondary market for mortgage contracts. This is what Fannie Mae and Freddie Mac do, and what you can do, but on a much smaller scale. Most lenders don't hold the loans they make for the duration. They sell those loans on the secondary market to organizations like Fannie and Freddie, and then the lenders are able to use the proceeds to make more loans.

But remember, not all loans are lender-originated. There are thousands of private mortgages out there at any given time. For example, a seller may sell a piece of property on "land contract" to a buyer, meaning that a private mortgage exists between buyer and seller. Alternately, a seller may carry a second mortgage directly, which makes it easier for the buyer to get a bank loan for the bulk of the price. In the latter case, a lender may issue a mortgage for 80 percent of the purchase price, and the seller carries the other 20 percent directly. The simple strategy here is that you buy these private mortgage contracts. You don't ever have to see a single piece of real estate, and you don't have to go through the hassle of buying and selling property. You don't have to do any renovations. You're just a middleman.

This market exists because private individuals who hold such contracts often want to get all the cash out of their contract for one reason or another in one lump sum and are willing to sell the contract at a discount.

Most private mortgages, or "private paper" as some call it, carry a higher than average rate of interest, sometimes double the prevailing rate for "good credit" mortgages, making this an excellent place to park your money. You're gaining in two ways when you buy a private mortgage contract. First, you gain because you are buying a performing contract on which somebody is paying a high rate of interest. Second, you gain because you buy the contract at a discount.

$$$ *Part-Time Real Estate Investor Tip* $$$

When dealing in the secondary market in this way, remember that there is an actual piece of property behind the mortgage you are purchasing and do your own due diligence. Find out what the actual market value of the property is. It may well be that the person selling you the note has inflated the price to begin with. Find out about how well the note has been performing—that is, has the buyer of the property been paying the note on a timely basis, and for how long?

For example: Suppose somebody holds a private mortgage on which $100,000 is owed, and the mortgagee is paying monthly payments at 9 percent. When you buy the mortgage, you gain the right to receive those monthly payments of principal plus interest. But you buy the mortgage for less than face value. You may have purchased the contract for a 10 percent discount, or $90,000. That means not only do you receive the benefit of the 9 percent interest, but you also gain an additional $10,000, or the difference between the face value and your purchase price.

SELLING PURCHASE CONTRACTS

This strategy doesn't work in all locations. In our preferred target market of lower income or working class neighborhoods, you would certainly lose money. The strategy of buying and selling purchase contracts, rather than properties themselves, works only in a market that's "on fire."

Here's how it works. Suppose there is an upscale condo development being built in a high-priced beach town like Carmel, California. Let's assume too, that the price of real estate is rising rapidly there at the time. In this case, you actually just buy the right to purchase one of the condos. You can't buy the actual condo itself, because it doesn't exist yet. So after going through all the normal credit checks and contract dealings, you are able to put down a deposit of, say, $10,000. This gives you the right to purchase one of the condos at a fixed price when they are ready. It's sort of like the futures market, but instead of buying a future load of cocoa or soybeans, you're buying a future piece of real estate. In a market like Carmel, there is very little new construction going on, and real estate is in high demand. When you buy crude oil futures, for example, you are placing a gamble that the price of crude will increase beyond the price you paid. Your gamble here is that the market price of the condo will rise beyond the price on your contract. Suppose, for example, your contract gives you the right to buy the condo at $400,000, but before the construction is finished, they are almost completely sold and the market rate rises to $500,000. You can then sell your option, for which you paid $10,000, for a premium, and pocket the difference.

Naturally, there is a risk. When you invest in the stock market, the stock gurus tell you to spread your risk between different categories of stocks, putting a certain percentage into secure, sure bets and "blue chip" stocks, and a certain percentage into stocks that represent a higher risk but a higher potential reward. The same holds true for real estate investors. The strategy of selling purchase contracts is risky. The potential rewards are great, and there is very little work involved. Don't, under any circumstances, put your entire real estate investment capital into these sorts of investments—but consider using a small percent of your capital to speculate in this way.

CHAPTER 17

Negotiating Tactics

The first rule of negotiation is to never be afraid to ask for something outrageous.

If you're negotiating an owner-finance deal and they want $40,000 down, and you want to give them nothing down, put it out on the table. Maybe they'll turn you down, and maybe you'll meet somewhere in the middle. Or, maybe, they'll accept your offer.

Your goal is to acquire property for the least amount possible. Ideally, you want two things: (1) the lowest total price, and (2) the lowest amount of up-front capital requirement. Getting a low-priced property for only a few thousand dollars down is a lot different from getting a low-priced property and having to put $30,000 down or paying cash for the entire thing. It's true that the more you pay up-front, the smaller interest you will pay in the long run, but that's not the only consideration. There is also an opportunity cost involved. If you can acquire the property without having to pay much, then you have capital left to acquire additional properties and build your empire.

LOOK FOR CONCESSIONS

By gaining a good understanding of the property, as well as the individual circumstances of the seller, you can often find several opportunities for asking for concessions. Here are a few examples:

- Your pre-purchase inspection reveals several cosmetic repairs that are necessary to make the house habitable. List these items and the approximate cost to make the repairs. Ask the seller to lower the price accordingly.

- The house has been on the market for a year, and the market in that neighborhood is soft. The seller is likely to be willing to accept a lower price.

- The house is vacant. Because it is not generating the seller any income and is probably costing them money to maintain, it has become a burden to them. They are losing money every day they own it. Ask for a lower price and creative financing.

- The seller has an existing mortgage that they are paying on every month, and it represents a burden to them. You can take over their mortgage, relieving them of their burden, and ask them to carry a second mortgage themselves for the balance.

- The seller needs money for some specific purpose. Find out precisely how much they need and what for and try to solve that problem for them.

- The sellers find themselves in hard financial times due to loss of a job, illness, divorce, or other problem. They need money, and they need it quickly. In such circumstances, the seller will very often sell the property for lower than market value.

NEGOTIATE FROM A POSITION OF POWER

Part of negotiation is a state of mind. Suppose, for example, that you are a relative beginner in real estate investment and you have very little in the way of assets, cash, and good credit. In such a case, you may feel that you have very little to bring to the table and have to take what's offered. This is not the case.

Do not enter into negotiations with the belief that you are inferior to your opponent in any way. If you do, you will feel intimidated by the other party and will not come out with a deal that is favorable to you. It doesn't matter if the other party is a multi-millionaire who could buy and sell you a hundred times over. You still must not have the state of mind of inferiority. You are your opponent's equal because you are both sitting down to negotiate over a deal that will benefit both of you in some way.

Even if you have no money whatsoever and your credit is too poor to allow you to walk into a bank without the security guard eyeballing you, you still have power when you enter into negotiations for a piece of property. Your power may simply be that you are offering to take a piece of property that the seller is having a hard time selling and that you are willing to meet their price if they will carry the mortgage with no money down.

$$$ *Part-Time Real Estate Investor Tip* $$$

Be willing to negotiate and don't enter into the deal with only one outcome in mind, but remember negotiating is a give and take process. If you give a concession, ask for something in return. Be willing to give a higher down payment, but in return, ask for a lower sales price. Raise your offering price, but ask for more favorable creative financing.

UNDERSTAND THE OTHER GUY'S NEEDS

I entered into a land contract to purchase a small "cracker-box" style home to live in for no money down. It was in a comfortable neighborhood and the price was reasonable. Later, the seller got into some financial trouble. She was trying to handle too many properties on too slim a margin and got in over her head. The bank called all of her loans and foreclosed. This meant trouble for me since the bank does not recognize any existing land contracts in case of foreclosure. They simply take ownership of the property and start from scratch.

I had been in my apartment in Bangkok for several months and had just returned to the States. One day, a strange man showed up at my door, unaware that I was even living there, and told me, "Hi, this is my house." Needless to say, it was a shock. I had been unaware of the foreclosure proceedings. He had apparently bought nearly 20 of the former owner's properties in a package deal, directly from the bank. Having been cut out of the loop, I was understandably a bit shaken by the turn of events. I attempted to negotiate another land contract with this individual, but he wasn't buying. He had a rigid set of standards and protocols and would only go through a conventional lender.

He was anxious to get into the house, do his small bit of renovation, and flip the property for a quick profit. I stalled for time while I looked for another house. I found one in the form of my current historic Victorian home which is about three times the size of the old one.

Here's the twist: He wanted me out as quickly as possible, because he was losing money every month on it. I wanted to recover at least a little of the money I had put into it. Now, at this time, I didn't tell him I had already found a new house, but I didn't tell him I hadn't either. I offered him a deal: I would move out immediately and turn over possession. This would allow him to get on with his project and take his profit. In return, he would write me a check. He agreed, and we both walked away with something we wanted.

Understanding what your opponent wants and needs is the first key to a successful negotiation. That's not to say that you will give him everything he wants, but having a detailed understanding of his position will help you in your negotiations.

WHO HAS THE MOST FLEXIBILITY?

Whichever party has the most power will be the one who walks away with the greatest win. Part of that power is flexibility. If you have some available cash, a line of credit, and equity in other properties, you have a lot of options for the method you use to finance a house, and you can negotiate from a standpoint of more power. If you have no money at all and no credit, you have very little power since you have only one thing to offer. That's not to say that no money down is a bad strategy, it's just one strategy. No-money-down deals work best when you are negotiating from a position of power. Asking for a no-money-down deal when you have no money is not as powerful as asking for a no-money-down deal when you actually have a pocket full of cash. That's because the cash gives you other alternatives — other possibilities and room for negotiation.

On the other hand, always try to determine how much flexibility the seller has, because this will give you an idea of his level of power. If the seller has a half dozen buyers who want the property, he has more flexibility and will take the best offer that is available. But, if the seller's property has been sitting vacant for a year, he has very little in the way of flexibility, and you are in the superior position. Something is better than nothing — and he is getting nothing from a vacant property. For this reason, do some research into the property and the seller. Find out how long the property has been vacant and whether the seller has reduced the price already. Find out about the market and how long it takes other properties in the neighborhood to sell and for how much. And if you can, find out all you can about the seller's own personal and business situation. Does he own a hundred properties or just one or two? If the property you want is just one in a very large portfolio, he may be better equipped to wait out the market. If he owns two properties, he may be in a more desperate situation to sell one of them.

Always be willing to walk away

And do it graciously. If you are not willing to walk away from a deal and make it known that you may do so, you will be seen as a desperate competitor, and your opponent will take advantage of you. If your opponent is unwilling to negotiate, let him know that you are looking at several other properties in the same area and you will be able to pick them up on more favorable terms.

However, when you do walk out, don't burn your bridges. Leave the door open for future negotiations. If you leave graciously, the seller may well decide a month later that he is not going to get any better offers than yours, and he will call you back.

I always had great fun with the "walk away" technique when buying goods in Bangkok—a city well known for vendors willing to negotiate—where I first got a good understanding of the procedure. When you ask the price of something at a vendor's stall in the bazaar, if you are a Westerner, the starting price will be high. If you are able to speak some Thai, the starting price will go down a little. If you have a Thai person accompanying you, then the starting price will go down even more. I would always start out by approaching the vendor and asking in Thai language what the price was. My wife, who is a native of Thailand, would be lurking around the corner. After a bit of discussion, she would appear, and drag me off to look at something else in another vendor's stall. Inevitably, the merchant would follow and finally offer the "Thai" price, which is what I was looking for in the first place.

CHAPTER 18

"Subject to" Clause

This technique involves buying a home subject to existing mortgages. It's a fabulous technique for buying a house quickly and easily without qualifying from a bank and usually with very little money down.

"Subject to" is a type of sales contract where a seller conveys a house to a buyer, subject to existing mortgages. The buyer usually does two things: pays the seller a small amount of cash in consideration for the deal and any existing equity and then takes over payments of the seller's mortgage. The seller's mortgage remains in the seller's name, but the buyer makes payments. If a seller has very little or no equity in a property, you can acquire properties using this technique usually for only a token amount of cash.

With a "subject to" deal, you gain control over a piece of property. However, actual ownership remains with the seller until all underlying mortgages have been paid off. You don't have to get a new mortgage. There are many advantages to buying this way, including:

- You don't have to credit qualify.
- You usually put little or no money down.
- You gain control over the property quickly.
- Risk is minimal — the seller retains all risk.

One possible downside is that as you are making timely payments, you are improving the seller's credit score, and not your own. However, you're an investor trying to make money. Credit building, if you need it, is secondary to your real estate business. The biggest possible downside is the risk of the seller's creditors putting a lien on the property, but this is a calculated risk that you decide to take based on your assessment of the seller's situation.

The "subject to" is incredibly simple. The seller simply deeds the property over to the buyer. This can be done regardless of any existing liens or mortgages.

SELLING ON "SUBJECT TO"

First, I'll let you in on a secret—it's great to buy "subject to," but you should avoid selling "subject to" whenever possible. Here's why: The "subject to" technique involves buying a house directly from a seller, subject to any underlying mortgages. That means that there are no changes in the underlying mortgages. You, the buyer, simply start making payments on the seller's mortgage. The seller's mortgage remains in the seller's name, even though you are the one making the payments. This is great for you, the buyer. But the seller assumes all the risk here. That's because if the buyer stops making payments, or falls behind, the seller is still responsible.

For the seller, this can be a double-edged sword. A seller in financial distress, who may be on the verge of foreclosure, can sell on a "subject to" contract to get out of immediate danger. If the buyer makes timely payments, credit bureaus see those payments as being made by the seller, not the buyer, and the buyer gets improved credit as a result through no effort of their own. In this case, seller and buyer both win. But if the buyer makes late payments, there is a strike against the seller's credit. Buyer wins, but seller loses.

Selling a house with a "subject to" contract can be useful under some circumstances.

$$$ *Part-Time Real Estate Investor Tip* $$$

Never sell a house on a "subject to" clause if you are in a desperate situation and just want to get out from under a property — because you're not really out from under it. If you do sell a property on these terms, you should be in a position to take it back and resume payments if necessary.

"SUBJECT TO" VERSUS LAND CONTRACT

"Subject to" is similar to a land contract since it is a contract entered into between a buyer and seller with no third-party lender as intermediary. However, it differs in one important way. With a land contract, the buyer pays the seller directly, and then the seller uses the proceeds to pay off any existing mortgages. With a "subject to," the buyer makes the seller's mortgage payments.

The advantage to the buyer is that the risk of the seller defaulting on an existing mortgage is minimized, since the buyer takes over control of the payments.

$$$ *Part-Time Real Estate Investor Tip* $$$

Keep in mind that for your contract to be legally binding, there must be some consideration. A strict no-money-down deal may not hold up in court. For this reason, even if you agree to take over payments with no money down, there should be a token cash payment of a hundred dollars or so made for consideration.

WHAT DOES THE BANK THINK?

In short, they don't need to know. This is strictly a contract between buyer and seller. Trying to bring the bank in on the deal would just complicate matters and should be avoided at all costs. The less the bank knows, the better! Since they are in the business of issuing loans, if they were to discover such a transaction, they would naturally try to force the buyer to get a new mortgage, since that means they would earn more points and fees. There is a possible risk of a bank trying to call a loan if they discover that a property has been sold "subject to" their mortgage, but in reality, the risk is minimal. So long as payments are being made on a timely basis, most lenders don't really care where the money is coming from.

There is such a thing as a "due on sale" clause, which is common with most mortgages. This simply says that the bank has the *right* to call the loan if the property changes hands. However, as a practical matter, even though the bank has this right, they will not execute that right unless there is a compelling reason to do so, and the most frequent compelling reason is that the note is not getting paid. If a bank's mortgage is a performing mortgage — that is, payments are being made every month and on a timely basis — the bank has very little reason to care whether a quitclaim deed has been filed. So long as you continue making your payments and aren't late, the risk here is very slim.

I note here that a "subject to" sale is not the same as a mortgage assumption. A mortgage assumption, which is very hard to come by, is a deal where a lender actually permits their mortgage to be assumed by a new owner without having to actually take out a new loan. The mortgage is formally transferred to the new owner by the bank. Think of a "subject to" sale as a sort of informal mortgage assumption.

WHY WOULD A SELLER ENTER INTO A "SUBJECT TO" CONTRACT?

There are many different reasons why someone would do this.

- Seller may be in danger of foreclosure and wishes to get out from under a property.

- Seller may have very poor credit and will benefit from your timely payments on the underlying mortgage.

- Seller may be having difficulty selling the property due to a soft market or need for renovations.

- Seller may need to move to take a new job and doesn't have time to stay and sell it in the conventional way.

- If seller has no equity, the only alternative may be to pay a real estate agent their commission out of pocket, an action that would make a conventional sale a losing deal.

$$$ *Part-Time Real Estate Investor Tip* $$$

Paperwork. Besides a private contract between the buyer and seller, the seller also signs over the deed to the property so that the buyer's name becomes associated with it. The seller will execute a quit claim deed or warranty deed.

WHAT CAN YOU DO WITH THE PROPERTY ONCE YOU HAVE IT?

Once you have executed the "subject to" contract and the seller has signed a quitclaim deed, you can do what you want. You have complete control over the property. The first thing to do, as with any property, is to analyze what your monthly outflow will be and how much you need to spend on renovations. A few possibilities are:

- Use the property as a rental if rental revenue exceeds your outflow.

- Offer the property on a lease option, where your new tenants pay for the right to buy the property from you at a future date. You can do this even though you don't own the property free and clear, simply by doing two transactions at once when your tenants buy. Simply put, your tenants buy the property from you, and you pay off the existing mortgages and keep the difference between the two amounts as profit.

- Sell the property on a land contract.

- Sell the property outright to a person who can obtain third party financing. Use the proceeds of your sale to pay off the existing mortgages and keep the difference between the two amounts as profit.

THE QUITCLAIM DEED

This important but often misunderstood piece of paperwork is an important part of the "subject to" deal. Anyone can execute a quitclaim deed, even if there are underlying mortgages. Some sellers may not understand this and may think that they cannot sign such a document because they still have a mortgage on the property. However, it's just a simple tool that allows an owner to assign their rights to another person — in this case, you.

The quitclaim deed doesn't include any sort of guarantees about the title and doesn't address whether there are existing mortgages. It only assigns the claim and says that the sellers are assigning any rights they may have to the property, if any, to the buyer.

A warranty deed, on the other hand, means that the seller has clear title to the property. As such, the usual type of deed you will need to deal with when buying on a "subject to" contract is the quit claim deed.

Record your notarized deed with your local county office. The last deed that is recorded is the one that is considered to be in force, and this gives you a solid claim on the house. After that paper is signed, you actually own the house. You own it subject to the underlying mortgage, but you still own it. Don't confuse having this deed with having "clear title," which means there are no mortgages. Any office supply store can provide you with a blank deed form, which can be filled out between the two parties right on the kitchen table.

KNOW WHAT YOU ARE GETTING INTO

When you enter into a "subject to" deal, find out whether the seller is behind on mortgage payments. This is a very likely scenario and often why a seller is willing to sell it to you on these terms. Even so, it may still represent a good deal for both you and the seller. If the seller is behind on payments, it will be up to you to make up the arrearage, so figure that into your profit calculations.

This, of course, makes an attractive deal to sellers in trouble. Suppose a person is five months behind on a $1,000 a month mortgage and can't possibly come up with the $5,000 needed to get out of trouble. The person realizes they will have to move, and at this point they just want to make the phone calls stop. You pony up the $5,000 and start making payments on a timely basis.

CHAPTER 19

Other Types of Creative Financing

There are as many creative ways to buy a house as you can imagine. There are, of course, some homebuyers and investors who never think outside the box and confine themselves to whatever the bankers tell them. This thought process is no way to get rich.

Conventional, lender-based financing is only one out of many ways to buy a house. Of course, it is not something that should be ignored, and if you are able to get bank financing, it should definitely be one tool in your toolbox, but it shouldn't be the only one. Sometimes getting a conventional bank loan may be the best way to get a house, but on other occasions you can make a better deal, close quicker, and make more profits if you bypass the bank completely. Don't be afraid to cut the banker out of the loop.

Cash always works, and if you have access to it your chances of success increase exponentially. Very few sellers will turn down a cash deal. Many of the creative alternatives discussed in this book and elsewhere don't appeal to everybody and won't always work, but that doesn't mean they are useless. They don't have to work every time for you to be successful.

The main creative ways of buying a house I've discussed in this book so far include owner financing (land contract), lease-purchase, the "subject to" contract, and tax lien sales. Here are a few other concepts.

THE FALLACY OF "OWN IT FREE AND CLEAR"

A real estate investor needs to get over the "I own it free and clear" mindset. Owning a piece of real estate free and clear with no underlying mortgages naturally has the advantage of (1) not having to make payments, and (2) having an asset that you can leverage for other purposes. But this is by no means the holy grail of real estate. Real estate debt to an investor is not necessarily a bad thing. So long as you have more coming in than you have going out, you are successful.

Similarly, many people turn up their nose at the idea of buying a property without a large down payment. They think buying an investment property with little or no money down is unwise because you actually own less of the property and your mortgage payments will be higher.

There are two important things in making a real estate deal: (1) gaining control over a piece of real estate and (2) making money. You don't need a large equity stake in the property to do these things. As to item No. 1, gaining control over a piece of real estate doesn't necessarily mean you need put much money into it. As I've outlined previously, there are several different ways you can gain control over a piece of property without having to put down any money at all. What matters is that once you have control over the property, you can use it to your advantage to make money. Let's take a closer look at this philosophy. Suppose you take a strategy of 20 percent down, because you listened to your banker. You have $40,000 to invest, and so you buy a $200,000 house as an investment. You are therefore able to take control over one house.

Now if you have control over one house, you are subject to a lot of "what if" situations. What if the house stays on the market longer than you planned? What if the market goes soft and you can't resell it for as much as you figured? Then you lose. But, by diversifying and spreading out your risk, you will do better. Gaining control over 10 houses is better than having control over one. If you have 10 houses, and one of them doesn't sell at a profit, you still have nine others that may. You haven't lost everything. Instead of taking that $40,000 and buying a single house conventionally, make 10 creative deals (without the bank's help), and your risk has been lowered dramatically. You can see that while bankers like to make you think that they know the most risk-free way of doing business, *doing it the conventional way is actually riskier.*

Having said all that, an excellent strategy is to own one property free and clear (or at least have a substantial amount of equity in it) and then use that equity to obtain other homes without having to use any out of pocket cash. Owning one house free and clear and using that property to buy a dozen other homes "on the margin" is a useful strategy indeed.

For example: Suppose you own a home free and clear, and its current value is $200,000. You can easily obtain a loan for 90 percent of that value, and then you will have a stockpile of cash that you can use to make more deals. When making your creative deals, although "no money down" is always good, many deals will take a little cash to prime the pump, so to speak. You may need a few thousand to make a deal happen, pay off the seller's debts, do repairs, or make mortgage payments while the house is being renovated.

CASH BACK AT CLOSING

This is one of those deals the real estate gurus like to boast about in their expensive seminars, but it almost never happens. Nonetheless, here it is for what it's worth. It requires a desperate seller who has a house with no equity and who needs out from under it quickly. It also requires the seller not to be behind on mortgage payments.

The logic of the deal is this: The seller has no equity, and if they were to sell it through conventional methods, they would have to pay a real estate agent's commission out of pocket. That could be substantial, often amounting to 6 percent or more of the sale price. Further, it requires the seller to be willing to sell you the house using a "subject to" private contract, and there must not be a real estate agent involved. The deal that you, as an investor, are offering the seller is to relieve the seller of the burden of the expenses involved in selling the house. In exchange, you get some of the money that the seller saves.

You buy the house from the seller on the "subject to" contract. You take over payments immediately, and the seller is then relieved of the burden and can move on with their life. The seller does not have to pay the real estate agent commissions and other marketing expenses, and so the seller agrees to split the difference with you. For example, suppose commissions and other marketing expenses would have totaled $10,000. Instead, the seller pays you $5,000, and then both you and the seller are $5,000 ahead of the game. You can point out to the seller that they may even be further ahead than that. Suppose it takes an average of six months to sell a house in your area, so that means they would have to shoulder the burden of making mortgage payments for six additional months, in addition to the sales expenses.

How do you convince a seller to pay you $5,000 for the privilege of buying their house? That's the $5,000 question, and the answer is, most of the time you won't be able to, even though on paper it looks good. But in a few rare cases, this is actually a good deal for the seller, because they may well wind up losing more money by not paying you.

SELLING AT ABOVE MARKET

An arbitrageur is someone who deals in financial markets and takes advantage of relative differences in prices, usually of equities or some sort of derivative vehicle. You as a real estate investor can profit through something similar to arbitrage.

The short explanation is that you use your best negotiating techniques to purchase a piece of property with as little money down as possible for the lowest price you can haggle. You then sell it on creative terms to a buyer for an above market rate.

You must realize that there are two different types of people who buy real estate on creative terms. You are one—an investor who is simply trying to create a business and make the most profit possible. The other type of buyer is one who is not looking for an investment but rather wants to buy a home to live in and doesn't have access to traditional, mainstream banking methods of finance. You as an investor, especially if you have several houses under your control already, have a great deal of leverage, power, and real estate savvy to make the best deal possible. Your primary motivation in selecting a property is to select one that will generate a profit. Your monthly outflow will be less than your monthly income. The other type of owner, however, isn't as interested in profit: They want a home. As such, they are not constricted by price as much as you are. However, they are constricted by other factors such as poor credit, not enough down payment, or some other reason so that they cannot get a conventional loan. Because they are so constricted, they are willing to pay above market rates for a home if you offer it to them on favorable terms.

Here's a quick example. Suppose you find a modest home in a working-class neighborhood. It needs a little cosmetic work. The seller wants $75,000 for it, and you eventually settle for $70,000, on a "subject to" contract where you take over mortgage payments, and the seller carries back a second mortgage directly for the balance. You also give the seller a $3,000 cash down payment, and you also put $2,000 and a little time into cosmetic repairs, paint, and lawn maintenance and landscaping. Your total initial outlay is $5,000. Your monthly outflow looks something like this:

Underlying mortgage	$400
Seller mortgage	$200
Taxes and insurance	$100
Total	$700

Through advertising, you meet a young couple. Although they have not been on the job for long, they both have reasonably good jobs, and they are new in town. They want to buy a home, but they have had some credit problems in the past so that banks won't talk to them. The couple did talk to one subprime lender, but the lender would only deal with them if they were able to make a 20 percent down payment and then pay 18 percent interest. You decide they are a good risk. They like the house, and you offer it to them for $85,000, about 20 percent above your purchase price. They don't have a lot to put down but are able to get together $5,000, which you decide to accept, and you agree to carry a land contract (or "wrap around" mortgage) for the $80,000 balance, at 10 percent—above the current bank rates, but below what could be considered usurious rates. They also will pay the taxes and insurance to you, and you will handle these payments. Your monthly income will be about $800 from this property, and you have also earned back the $5,000 you put out to acquire the property. Your situation now is that you are out no money at all, and you have a $100-a-month profit.

Granted, $100 a month isn't much (and this is just an example), but consider that once the deal is made you are out nothing in terms of net out-of-pocket expense. If you repeat this same deal multiple times, it starts to add up. Also there is another consideration here: You are giving the buyers a 30-year contract. The mortgages that you are handling, however, are less than that. Suppose, for example, that there are 10 years left on the underlying bank mortgage and the seller mortgage is also a 10-year note. After 10 years, your monthly profit increases by $600!

PART THREE

THE NUTS AND BOLTS

CHAPTER 20

Conventional Mortgages

There are many creative ways to buy a house and get financing, and those techniques should be part of any investor's handbook. If you don't have good credit or a lot of cash, creative financing may be the only way you can get into the business. Despite this fact, along with my earlier warnings about bankers, don't be so quick to dismiss them entirely. There may be some circumstances when working with traditional banks can be in your best interest.

Many banks remain willing to work with people to finance the purchase of an investment property. They understand that many investors will no doubt prove to be good loan customers. But the terms (unless perhaps you are buying as an owner-occupant initially) will be starkly different in most cases. Obviously, a loan for an investment property will carry a higher interest rates and require a larger down payment, usually 20 percent at a minimum, as mortgage insurance is not available for such properties.

CREDIT RATING

No matter how you arrange your financing, eventually you have to pay off the house one way or another. Creative financing may be the only way to get your foot in the door, but it is also more likely to yield higher payments and more interest. By all means, if you are credit challenged, as an increasingly large percentage of Americans are today, go for the creative financing. Do anything you can do to start acquiring real estate, but at the same time, work on your credit by amassing equity in your properties.

I'll dispense with the other "clean up your credit" claptrap. You all know that you should pay your bills on time, and that's the subject of another book. But one important thing to know about good credit: there is the numeric score, and there is the *de facto* score. There are factors that come into play that are not in your credit score. If your golf buddy is the loan officer, that's a factor. But the biggest factor of all is how much equity you may hold. If you have equity, your *de facto* credit improves. So apart from all the other traditional sound advice such as paying off your credit cards, avoiding payroll advance loans, and driving a modest automobile, the best credit advice I can give you is to create equity in property. If two people with a similarly marginal credit rating and similar amount of available cash both apply for a bank loan, and one has $25,000 in real estate equity and the other has none, guess which one will get the loan? A banker who sees equity is much more likely to overlook the fact that you've been naughty with your credit cards. That's not to say he won't charge you more interest for your sins, but you will get the loan.

$$$ *Part-Time Real Estate Investor Tip* $$$

Don't be afraid of bankers. Conventional mortgages can serve your needs well, but on the other hand, don't be closed-minded. Stay open to creative concepts of acquisition and financing regardless of how great your credit may be. Those who believe that bankers and conventional mortgages are the only way to go are those who miss out on some of the best opportunities.

Realize that in creative, owner-finance schemes, the seller typically charges several interest percentage points above what the bank will charge. If you're in the driver's seat—that is, if you're the one selling—this is great for you. As I discussed in the last section, *selling* property using creative techniques gives you *two* profit centers: the profit you make from the difference between your buy and sell prices and the interest income your buyer will give you. However, interest over the course of a 30-year loan far exceeds the actual price of the real estate itself. If you can get your property a couple of percentage points cheaper, you can save an enormous amount of money.

Here's an example. Suppose you want to finance $300,000 to buy a property and are able to put $50,000 down (a healthy amount to impress the lender). Suppose, also, that the mortgage lender offers you a rate of 5 percent. Let's assume the property tax is 1.25 percent and homeowners insurance will cost $1,000 a year. Your monthly principal and interest will come to $1,737.89. Over the course of a 30-year loan, you will repay the principal of $250,000, and you will also pay total interest in the amount of $233,139.46. Now, let's take a deal that carries an 8 percent interest rate. Your monthly jumps up to $2230.24, and the total interest over 30 years comes to a whopping $410,388.12. Of course, the bank is going to charge you some "points," but even if that comes to $3,000 or $4,000, the overall impact is still the same. A difference of 3 percent can make the difference between profit and loss. Besides the bottom-line amount, the monthly amount can also seriously impact your cash flow. If you're using the home as a rental and the market rate is $900 a month, you're going to be operating too close to the margin at the 8 percent rate, but you will have some good cash flow at the 5 percent rate.

MORTGAGE RATES

If you do decide that a conventional mortgage is going to be the best thing for your investment plan, then you should become familiar with a few things. The first thing you'll notice is that the interest rate will vary between banks and maybe even between cities. Those great rates that the lenders advertise in the papers are just for people who intend to buy residences. After they run your application, they may offer you a loan that's not quite as attractive as you thought you would get. How they arrive at the rate they offer you is a bit of a mystery. Then you also have to take into account the closing costs and "points" that can also have a big impact on your bottom line.

When you decide to use mortgage lenders, you should also become familiar with a governmental entity known as the Federal Reserve Board. Its decisions affect the rate lenders offer. Understanding what the "Fed" is doing and what they are likely to do in the near future is important. Economists may, for example, believe that the Fed may raise (or lower) the interest rate at their next monthly meeting, and that's good information to know. If you believe the Fed may lower the rate, you may want to wait until that happens to get a better interest rate. On the other hand, if you think they may raise it, you'll want to lock in a lower rate right away.

$$$ *Part-Time Real Estate Investor Tip* $$$

Interest rates are contrary to the strength of the economy. That is, if the economy is strong, the Fed will raise the interest rate to avoid inflation; if the economy is weak, the Fed will lower it to stimulate the economy. In so doing, the nation's economy stays in balance. In recent years, interest rates have fallen to historic lows. When the Fed will begin to nudge rates higher remains a topic of debate.

The Fed doesn't actually set the interest rates for the banks. Banks are free within a broad set of guidelines to charge what they will. The Fed sets a "Federal Funds Rate," which is the interest rate on overnight loans between the Federal Reserve and other banks. Mortgage rates are then derived from that Federal Funds rate.

Adjustable and fixed

An adjustable rate mortgage (ARM) has a rate of interest that can vary over the life of the mortgage. Depending on the economy and your personal circumstances, these may or may not be a good thing for you. Typically, an ARM gives you an introductory rate that is lower than the rate you would get on a fixed loan, but don't be lulled into a false sense of benefit here: That's an introductory rate only. It's like the cable company that gives you cable TV at half price for the first month. That loan will go up after the first six months or year to reflect the current market rate.

If the economy is weak and the interest rates are, therefore, low to begin with, a fixed rate loan is probably going to be better in the long run. But if the economy is strong and interest rates are high, the adjustable deal will give you a better deal in the long run, because the rates will go down when the economy weakens.

Bad credit conventional mortgages

Investors with impaired credit are better off seeking some of the alternative, creative financing methods discussed in this book; but even if you have bad credit, you shouldn't write the bankers off entirely. Keep your options open and know what you have available to you. The bankers may not want to do business with you at all, but you may be surprised.

$$$ *Part-Time Real Estate Investor Tip* $$$

D on't make the mistake of believing that you need flawless credit to get a mortgage. You only need flawless credit to get a mortgage at the best advertised rate.

Subprime loans

The term "subprime loan" still haunts the real estate industry. So-called subprime lenders were all the range in the run-up to the real estate crash of 2008, which lingered for many years afterward, taking down real estate values across the country. Most experts say that a phenomenal surge in subprime loan activity — loans that were made to people who did not qualify for conventional loans — helped usher in the real estate crash. There were lots of controversial loans being made at the time — subprime and others, like so called stated income loans — that in hindsight made a mockery of traditional mortgage lending. That period in economic history continues to fascinate people. A well-reviewed movie was made about that era, The Big Short, starring Brad Pitt. It was nominated for a best-picture Oscar in 2016.

Given that subprime loans were aimed at people who had specific mortgage challenges, it's only natural to wonder if these loans might be appropriate for investment property purchased. It's a great question — one with an easy answer: look elsewhere. The regulatory and market crackdown in the wake of the real estate crisis pushed many subprime operations out of business. Just recently, such loans have been making a comeback of sorts. But these days, the loans are extended more for auto purchases and for small businesses than for property purchases.

Equity and mortgages

Bad credit becomes less relevant if you already have equity in property. If you own a $100,000 house free and clear, you can find a lender to deal with you, regardless of how bad your credit may be. That's why your initial strategy in your beginning years as an investor is not just to turn a quick profit but to build equity for the long run, which you can leverage later on to make more deals.

Naturally, there is a risk involved, but that's the nature of doing business. There is always going to be a risk. There is no "sure thing," even in real estate—no matter what the real estate gurus tell you. The risk in getting an equity loan is that if you default on the loan, the lender can take the property you used as equity to get the loan. That said, there are still advantages. Besides being easy to get, you can use funds from an equity loan for both buying additional properties and for making renovations. Indeed, many banks seem to prefer extending home equity loans for this purpose, as opposed to issuing a new standalone mortgage.

Mortgage brokers

A large number of mortgage loans are initiated by a mortgage broker rather than the lender directly. A mortgage broker is a middleman who simply arranges the deal. In an ideal world, the broker will have connections to several lenders and will be in a position to know where you will get the best deal. A good broker may even be aware of deals that you as an individual investor would not be aware of, and in such a case the broker fee would be well worthwhile.

But brokers are not bound by precisely the same laws as lenders, and they make a bigger profit if they sell you a mortgage that is less advantageous to you. Depending on the state you live in, mortgage brokers may be under no regulations whatsoever. More states are imposing licensing requirements on brokers, so it pays to find out what those requirements are and to do a little due diligence on a broker before doing business with them. The best broker is one with connections who is very familiar with the financial services industry as well as the real estate industry.

CHAPTER 21

Titles and Paperwork

More than most, real estate has a paperwork burden, and you have to make sure you have all your ducks in a row. There's paperwork for the city or county, for the mortgage lender, for the real estate agent, and everybody else involved in the process.

Keep in mind that no matter how diligent you may be or how much you may trust the other party, you still must put everything in writing, make it official, and document everything. There's big money involved in real estate, and any time there is big money involved, some people will show their worst side. There is an increased risk of fraud and an increased risk of other people trying to take advantage of you. Here's an example of how things can go wrong: A librarian friend of mine and his wife wanted to move to a different school district and found a house they liked in the right area. It looked good when they first saw it, and they made an offer with an earnest money check. Naturally, it was a standard offer with a "subject to inspection" clause, which means that my friend promised to buy the house, assuming it would pass a third party inspection.

The house did not pass. Although cosmetically it looked fine, there were bigger problems, and my friend withdrew his offer. The sellers (who seemed to be a little desperate) tried to hold them to the agreement, saying that if they made the necessary improvements, then my friend would still be bound to buy the house. My friend correctly refused to go along with it, saying that since it did not pass, he had the right to back out. A bitter fight ensued, and my friend ended up losing his earnest money deposit. He could have taken the issue to court and won but decided to cut his losses, since his time (and the money he would have spent on lawyers) outweighed the smaller deposit at issue. The point here is, when there is money involved, trust no one. Never assume that everything will go as it should.

What does the lender want you to have?

Needless to say, when you are working with a conventional lender, you will need a substantial amount of paperwork and other assorted requirements. Foremost is the credit report, so become very familiar with your credit report ahead of time, because everybody will want to see it. Your FICO score is a rating derived by the credit reporting agency. It's a single number that most mortgage lenders live by. Be aware that the information on your credit report changes every month, and as a result, so does your FICO score. The highest numeric score is 900, and if you have that score, bankers will be lining up to give you money. If it's below 620, it's considered poor, and mainstream lenders will give you the bum's rush out the door.

But besides your FICO score, the lender will also want to know about your debt-to-income ratio, so be prepared with copies of all of your credit card statements, car payments, and other loans to show what the total amounts are, what the monthly payments are, and whether you have been paying on a timely basis. Have your account numbers handy. In an ideal world, the lender wants to see a debt-to-income ratio of no more than 15 percent. That is, outside of your primary mortgage, you shouldn't be spending more than 15 percent of your take-home pay on credit cards, car payments, and the like. Some lenders may even ask you to pay down some of your existing debt before they will grant you a home loan.

Also, if you are employed, come to your meeting with information about your employer, including check stubs, and all relevant dates—they will want to know exactly how long you have worked there and how much you earn.

$$$ *Part-Time Real Estate Investor Tip* $$$

When dealing with banks, you can never have too much paperwork on hand.

Also, any assets that you have will have to be listed, and you will need documentation. Putting down on the application that you have $25,000 in the bank isn't good enough, you'll need bank statements proving that. And more than likely, you'll need something along the lines of six months' worth of bank statements so you can prove to the bank that you didn't just borrow the money from someone else to make it look like you have more than you really do.

STAYING ON THE RIGHT SIDE OF THE LAW

Any time you facilitate a real estate deal for someone else, you're acting as a broker, and you are then subject to an endless array of laws and regulations. To act in this way—that is, to facilitate a deal for a third party—you have to be a licensed real estate broker. If you aren't licensed, and you facilitate such a deal, you're stepping on the toes of a powerful lobby, so watch out! If you act as a middleman and accept any type of compensation, you could be subject to fines or even criminal prosecution in some states.

However, the state real estate commission does not have any jurisdiction if you are making real estate deals on your own behalf, and you do not have to be licensed, regardless of your state of residence. That's just horse-trading, and anybody can do it without any license and without any licensed third parties. The real estate brokers may not like it (and why should they, if you're cutting them out of the action!), but it's your deal, and you can involve or exclude whomever you wish.

There are, of course, some regulations to which you will have to adhere, whether you are a broker or not. The Fair Housing Act says you can't discriminate in either the sale or rental of property, based on somebody's race or color, national origin, religion, sex, family status, or handicap. There are a handful of exemptions to this act, but for the most part, if you are an investor, the exceptions won't apply to you, so it's best to get familiar with the act from the beginning and adapt your policies accordingly. If you're a small-time landlord with three or fewer single-family houses, and you're not using the services of a licensed real estate professional (who will be bound by the act at all times, regardless of your own status), you are exempt. Also, if you have an apartment building with four or fewer units, and if you live in one of them, you are exempt.

You will also have to comply with the Residential Lead-Based Paint Hazard Reduction Act. Any time to execute a sale or rental of a property build prior to 1978, you have to include a disclosure statement on the hazards of lead-based paint as to whether you have any knowledge of lead-based paint in the property.

WHAT IS A MORTGAGE?

There is always a little confusion about the term "mortgage." A mortgage is not exclusively a banking document. Banks certainly issue and hold mortgages, but they are not the only ones who can do so. A mortgage is merely a term used to describe the negotiable document that says one party is borrowing money from a second party and that loan is secured by real estate. If you sell a piece of property by land contract, you are the holder of a mortgage.

Almost all mortgages issued by banks contain a "due on sale" clause, and this is something to be aware of, especially if you plan to sell a property on land contract while you still have a mortgage on it. A due-on-sale clause gives the lender authority to make the loan due immediately if the property is sold without the lender's permission. The reality of the situation is that so long as payments are being made, the bank is not likely to call in the loan. Nonetheless, you should know whether this clause is in your contract.

However, there are ways to protect yourself, whether you are buying or selling. If you buy real estate directly from a seller on a land contract or other sort of installment deal, the seller should sign all title transfer paperwork, such as a warranty deed, and then put them in escrow with an escrow or title company. Ideally, it's best to do all of the transactions through an escrow company because this provides further documentation as to the legitimacy of the transaction. Doing so will also avoid ugly situations where you make payments to the seller but the seller doesn't pay off their own underlying mortgage. In other words, you make your land contract payments to an escrow company and the escrow company makes payments on the seller's underlying mortgages and then gives the seller the remainder every month.

$$$ *Part-Time Real Estate Investor Tip* $$$

When buying on a "subject to" contract or land contract arrangement, it's best for the seller to maintain property insurance and for you to pay the seller. That way, the hazard insurance stays in the name of the person who actually holds the underlying mortgage. If you take out insurance in your own name, it's possible that the underlying mortgage holder will get wind of it, and this may cause them to decide to call the loan.

RENTAL AND LEASE AGREEMENTS

If you are buying properties to rent or lease out, make sure you have a good rental/lease agreement handy. Many landlords make the mistake of just grabbing the "standard" lease available at the stationery store without even reviewing it.

The first thing to do is to consider your own needs in the rental agreement. For example, suppose you buy the house next door to where you live. Naturally, you will want quiet tenants. If (as is my own dilemma, unfortunately) your neighbor has endless backyard barbecue parties and plays deafening rap music under the mistaken impression that the entire block wants to hear it, you could have some remedies if you were that person's landlord. A clause in the lease should specifically address the tenant's behavior and should lay out specifically that loud music is not to be played at any time.

Similarly, if appearance of the property is important to you, make sure to put in a maintenance clause, which states that the tenant is responsible for things like lawn care and keeping the property free from trash and debris—and that failure to do so is cause for eviction.

Another item to consider is to require the tenant to list all residents who will be living in the house. This will prevent situations where your tenant brings in their sisters, cousins, aunts, uncles, and all their kids, and you end up with twenty people living in your house.

Of course, you want to get your money on time every month. How strict you are is a matter of personal choice, but any good lease agreement will have a provision for late fees; for example, if rent is more than five days late, the tenant must pay a $50 late fee. On the other hand, you can reverse that, and offer a discount for timely payment. Either way, it works out the same.

Understand in detail any tenants' rights laws in your state or city. Some cities have laws that are very restrictive to landlords and favor tenants exclusively, and these sorts of laws can make landlording very unprofitable indeed. It may, for example, take several months to evict a non-paying or undesirable tenant, because of convoluted tenants' rights laws. Landlords will often resort to simply paying off the bad tenant to get them to agree to go away. This is why very few people want to go into the landlording business in places like Berkeley, for example.

CHAPTER 22

For Sale by Owner

Real estate agents, like bankers, want to be your friend. Use their services sparingly and only when absolutely necessary.

$$$ *Part-Time Real Estate Investor Tip* $$$

Real estate agents are usually able to sell a property much faster than you would be able to sell it yourself. For the most part, this is because they are better connected and have more resources at their disposal. Besides just listing a property in the classifieds, they often have a vast network of previous customers, banking connections, and others. Most average buyers will look to real estate agents first, and so those agents will naturally have a large collection of ready buyers at any given time.

Before I become accused of slamming real estate agents, let me say that they are quite knowledgeable and can be very helpful in many circumstances. For individuals (not investors) buying or selling a home, their ability to guide you through the maze of real estate dealings can be valuable. But when you are an investor and are trying to maximize your profits, you must consider yourself the professional. The 6 percent commission charged by the agent may well be worthwhile to the lay individual, but it simply eats into an investor's profit. Moreover, the need to pay the agent's commission up-front completely eliminates any possibility of a no-money-down deal.

SELLING IT YOURSELF

Although selling your property yourself is usually the best option if you are an investor trying to make the most money possible, there are some obstacles. Having somebody else do it for you is always going to be easier, but nobody ever said that making huge profits was going to be easy.

One of the biggest advantages to *not* selling it yourself is the simple fact that a real estate agent is probably going to be more familiar with the market and will be able to pinpoint more accurately how much the property will sell for and how quickly. Of course, if you are an investor that has a large volume of real estate, you too will become familiar with the market and will have just as good a sense of it as the real estate agent. But if you're just starting out or only have a few properties, this may be a problem, and you may easily misjudge the market and price your property either too high or too low.

Real estate agents trying to get your business will speak of the opportunity cost of selling it yourself, and they have a valid point. The opportunity cost involves the time you could be spending doing something other than trying to sell your property. And if buying and selling property is not your main business, your time may well be better spent working on something else. It will take time to create and place your ads, and it will take time to show the property. Let's say that your main line of business is running a dot-com operation, and you're raking in big money there. You don't really want to take time out of that dot-com business to show property. But, if you want to be a successful real estate investor, buying and selling property *is* your business, so the opportunity cost equation does not apply.

Selling without benefit of an agent has a number of advantages. First of all, you will have more flexibility in terms of creative financing. Selling properties on land contract as opposed to conventional financing gives you the greatest return. Remember that when you are selling on these terms, you are acting as the lender as well as the seller, so you get money from two separate avenues: from the sale itself and from the interest you will charge. Typically, land contract sales carry a much higher interest rate than conventional loans, because you are usually selling to individuals that have some sort of credit challenge. But because you still have claim to the property if they default, you are still protected. You can easily write a land contract that is 3 to 6 percent higher than the current mortgage rate. For example, if bank mortgages are going for 7 percent, you can charge between 10 and 13 percent. There aren't that many places where you can get 10 percent on your money these days!

BUYING FSBOS AS OPPOSED TO LISTED PROPERTIES

Finding properties is one of the biggest challenges you'll face as an investor. True enough, there are hundreds of properties listed, but the ability to find the *right* one is what is going to get you rich. If you're just looking for a house to live in, you'll have a certain set of criteria, but when you're looking for a house that will make you money, there are a lot of different requirements. Naturally, you want to find properties that are selling for the lowest price to make the maximum profit.

$$$ *Part-Time Real Estate Investor Tip* $$$

There's a reason why you won't find the best bargains from your agent. It's because the agents keep those deals for themselves.

When a real estate agent lists a property, it's their job to get the highest price they can for it. Now when you're buying a single house to live in, the agent can be useful to your search because they are more likely to be able to find exactly what you want. But when you're an investor, everything is different. Profit is everything, and so you want the lowest price you can find. You won't find the best bargains from your local agent.

Professional investors don't limit themselves to buying properties that are listed through agents. If you want to make the big money, you have to do a little more work than that. Here are some of the more common places successful real estate investors find properties that make them money:

- FSBO properties listed on well-known websites such as **www
  .forsalebyowner.com, www.fsbo.com, www.homesbyowner
  .com, www.byowner.com,** and **www.zillow.com/
  for-sale-by-owner**.

- Newspaper classifieds online.

- Tax auctions and sheriff's sales.

- REO properties owned by banks or mortgage companies.

- Placing your own "we buy real estate" ad.

If you're not working through an agent (and most of the time, you shouldn't be), you have to make yourself known and make it possible for people with houses to sell to find you. After a while, you will get a reputation and become known, and you'll get some business via word-of-mouth. But, at first, signs and classified ads work very well. Try creating some classified ads and fliers with several different slogans. Here's a common one: "Avoid foreclosure! We buy houses fast." An ad like this will get you calls from people in financial trouble who may not have the time or luxury to work through an agent—or they may not be able to work through an agent because they have no equity and cannot afford to pay the commission out of pocket.

Placing such ads will take some time, and you will have to field a lot of calls that won't go anywhere, but you will also get some deals that work out. The advantage is that people are coming to *you* as the expert and not an agent. You have all the negotiating power. When you get a call from one of these ads, try to find out what the person's situation is. Ideally, they will be near foreclosure, will want out of their deal fast, and will have little or no equity in the property. You will be in a good position to offer a "subject to" deal where you just step in and take over their mortgages and pay their back payments for them.

You will no doubt get a lot of objections when you make offers like this, but remember that you have the upper hand, and they are calling you because they are in trouble. Even if they turn you down at first, chances are they are not going to get any better offers any time soon, and they may well call you back—so don't burn your bridges when they say "no deal." If they turn you down, keep their phone numbers and follow up in a few weeks with another phone call. Ask them politely if they have been able to resolve their situation and give them another opportunity to reconsider your offer. Sometimes it takes two or three tries, but as the seller gets more desperate and further behind, they are much more likely to consider a creative offer.

WORKING WITH A REAL ESTATE AGENT

There are two things to take into account when selling your property through a real estate agent: the sales commission they will charge and the services that they can provide. On the upside, if you are a newbie and don't have a lot of knowledge or connections, working with a real estate agent will give you these vital advantages. It will eat into your profits, but in the beginning this may be a necessary expense. Think of it as the cost of education. Working closely with a friendly agent will give you the advantage not only of services, but you can also get an education and see first-hand how the process works and what is involved. In this way, you can prepare yourself to make future deals without the benefit of the agent.

Since you're in the business of making deals, don't hesitate to try to make deals with real estate agents. Sure, many will be inflexible and won't budge on their 6 percent cut. But often, that 6 percent will be a deal breaker, cutting too much into your profit. The wise real estate agent realizes this and also realizes that working with a successful investor — even at half the commission — will be profitable for them. Don't be afraid to ask the agent to work with you on a lower commission structure.

Promoting your property is also easier with the help of an agent. Of course, it's a simple matter to put up a sign and take out a classified ad, but a real estate agent has access to something called the Multiple Listing Service (MLS), which gives you the greatest exposure possible.

Another hidden factor here is that real estate agents also tend to be well-connected to financing sources and will be more readily able to help your buyers obtain financing. If you're not doing owner-financing, the real estate agent will be very helpful in this regard.

$$$ *Part-Time Real Estate Investor Tip* $$$

Do you need the MLS or not? Decide ahead of time whether it will be advantageous to you. If you are selling properties on land contract or lease-option, it may be less essential, because buyers who want to buy on these sorts of terms will seek you out more aggressively — simply because properties being sold on these more creative terms are less likely to be listed through agents.

BEING A REAL ESTATE AGENT YOURSELF

The most advantageous strategy is to have the best of both worlds and be both an investor and an agent. If you are an agent yourself you'll have access to the MLS, which in itself is quite valuable and totally inaccessible to non-agents.

Some of the most successful agents don't actually even do that much selling on other people's behalf; rather, they spend most of their time working on their own properties. This gives you a foot in both camps—as a licensed agent, you will have more credibility and you will get people coming to you who wouldn't otherwise do business with you. And, naturally, because becoming an agent requires a great deal of study, you will become more knowledgeable about the real estate business in the process of becoming an agent. Do be aware that it's not necessarily easy or quick; be prepared to commit some real time to studying and getting licensed.

CHAPTER 23

Getting the Most out of Your Taxes

There are some myths out there that need to be cleared up. There are a lot of stories about how real estate is such a great tax shelter. And it's true; there are some tax advantages. But I've heard many times about how rich people sell or rent out their properties at a loss so they can take the tax write-off. *This just doesn't make any sense.* It's not true. Anybody who purposely rents out a piece of property for a negative cash flow, just so they can take a tax break, isn't a very good businessperson. To be sure, you should arrange your taxes so that you pay the least amount possible and take advantages of any and all breaks to which you are entitled. But the name of the game is *profit,* and you want as much of it as possible. A loss is still a loss, no matter how you look at it. There's just no way you can lose money and come out ahead by taking a tax write-off unless you're cheating on your taxes.

I'm not a big fan of paying huge fees to people, but it may be necessary or even a good idea to spend money on a good tax accountant with real estate experience. The laws are convoluted and change often, so having someone who can keep you up to date on what you can write off can be money well spent. Indeed, fixing your taxes the right way can mean the difference between making a profit and suffering a loss.

CAPITAL GAINS TAX

There's a big difference between the amount of taxes you must pay on capital gains and the amount of taxes you pay on regular earnings (a paycheck). Capital gains are a beautiful thing not only because they help you to accumulate wealth, but also because you pay taxes on your capital gains at a lower rate than other income.

When we talk about the favorable capital gains tax rates, we're talking about *long-term* capital gains tax, or taxes on assets you have held for over a year. If you sell the asset before a year, you will be taxed on the capital gains at your regular income tax rate. But if you buy a piece of property and sell it 366 days later, you qualify for the capital gains tax rate. One way to avoid having to sit on a property for a year is to sell it on a lease-option with the option being executed after a year's time. When you are renting or lease-optioning a property, it is still in your name so you can take advantage of the lower tax rate and still get some cash flow while you're waiting your required year and a day to sell.

There are different capital gains tax rates, and although they are all lower than regular income tax, the exact number will vary depending on your regular income level. For 2016, the top capital gains tax rate is 20 percent, which applies to single tax filers with taxable income of more than $415,050 and to married couples filing jointly with taxable income of $466,950. For single filers with taxable income between $37,650 and $415,050, that capital gains tax rate is 15 percent. Couples filing jointly with taxable income between $75,300 and $466,950 also pay the 15 percent rate.

CAPITAL GAINS TAX EXCLUSION

The capital gains tax exclusion is a great thing for homeowners and is one of the best ideas the lawmakers in Washington have ever come up with. I don't say that lightly since I believe that lawmakers don't usually have good ideas. But don't make the mistake of thinking that you can use the exclusion with all of your investment properties. The intent of this exclusion was to benefit homeowners, not investors. However, there are still some circumstances under which you can take advantage of it.

The federal capital gains tax exclusion is used to apply to the sale of a taxpayer's principal residence. If you have lived in your home for 24 out of the past 60 months, you qualify for this amazing exemption. Basically, you can exclude as much as $250,000 from capital gains taxes if you are single and up to $500,000 if you are married. In other words, assuming you qualify, you can sell your home and earn a profit and then not have to pay taxes on that profit.

However, if you're an investor buying and selling hundreds of properties, forget about this deal. You're not going to get it. But if you're a small-time investor who may be living in your own investment properties, there's an angle here. Some investors buy and renovate properties one at a time and live in the property while they are renovating. Besides the obvious benefits, taking this path gives you the benefit of being able to use the capital gains tax exclusion. You can use this exemption *every two years*, which means that you can buy a fixer-upper, live in it for two years while you are renovating it, sell it for a profit, and then not pay any income tax on that profit. Then you can do it all over again.

Even if you own multiple investment properties, as long as you are living in one of them (for at least two years), you can take the exclusion. Mind you, you can't take the exclusion for all of your properties, just for the one you are living in as your principal residence. Note here that you may be called upon to prove that the home is your principal residence if you are taking the exemption. Usually, so long as your tax returns have the address of the residence on them, you receive your mail at the address, and the address is reflected on your driver's license and other forms of ID, you'll be fine.

Also, although you are required to live in the home for 24 out of 60 months, they don't have to be 24 consecutive months. If you live in the home for a year, then live elsewhere for a while and then return to live in it for another year, you still qualify.

$$$ *Part-Time Real Estate Investor Tip* $$$

There are two approaches to real estate investing with regard to taxes: make your deals and then sort out what you owe Uncle Sam, or make your deals with Uncle Sam in mind from the beginning. Understanding ahead of time what tax breaks or tax burdens will come with any given deal can make or break you.

TAX CREDITS

At any given time, there are several different tax credits that you, as a real estate investor, may be able to qualify for. A tax *credit*, as opposed to a tax *deduction*, means that you take the credit amount directly off of your tax bill. A deduction, on the other hand, reduces the amount of income on which you pay tax. For example, suppose you owe taxes of $10,000 and you have a tax credit of $1,000. That means you will owe $9,000 in taxes— you save $1,000. On the other hand, if you have a tax deduction for $1,000, and you are in the 15 percent tax bracket, then you will save $150.

Because a tax credit directly reduces your tax liability, it's just as good as money in your pocket.

Available credits change over time, and sometimes the rules are complicated, so be sure to do some research on what is available and how you can qualify to receive these valuable credits.

If you do rehabs and fixer-uppers, you're in luck. Not only are you going to turn a profit simply by virtue of fixing up a property and selling it at a higher price, but you're also going to get a tax credit. The IRS allows a "rehabilitation tax credit," which is a credit with a social goal: it is meant to encourage investors to put money into older, potentially troubled neighborhoods. You can take a ten percent credit for renovating buildings built before 1936, and 20 percent if it is a certified historic building. You can include all of the expenses you incur for renovation and restoration, but you may not include expenses for new construction or enlargement.

A variety of other tax credits are also available for things like creating affordable housing or housing for the elderly. You may also get some tax credits if you adapt a commercial building to meet the needs of the Americans with Disabilities Act. Tax credits may also be able to be carried forward to subsequent years and can even be bought and sold. Be sure to check with your local state taxing authority as well; tax credits aren't limited to the federal government. Many states have specific programs as well that you can take advantage of to lower your state taxes payable.

DEPRECIATION

Depreciation is an accounting term for writing off the value of an asset over several years. Residential properties can be depreciated over 27 ½ years and commercial property over 31 ½ years. You can depreciate property, but not the land on which it sits—land, unlike buildings, never wears out.

DEDUCTIONS

Not everything you spend on your property is deductible as an expense. Nonetheless, if you can take a tax credit or depreciate it, it's just as good. Generally, if you spend money to add some permanent value to your property, it is a capital expenditure and is not deductible as an expense (but is probably depreciable).

Most operating expenses are going to be deductible. Routine repairs and maintenance, upkeep such as lawn care, and supplies are deductible as operating expenses. Also, if you pay utilities on your rentals, this too is deductible as an expense. Property taxes and interest are also expensed, as will be any property insurance you carry.

Other legitimate expenses include travel, including a mileage allowance for driving back and forth to your property, advertising expenses, legal and accounting fees, costs for management services, and education. Things like seminars and trade journals, *and the cost of this book*, are legitimate educational deductions for a real estate investor.

PASSIVE LOSSES

There's always a catch somewhere, and in the real estate investment business, this is it. The IRS enacted "passive loss" rules to prevent people with high incomes from using depreciation as a tax shelter. Generally, a passive investor is considered one who does not take an operational role in the real estate business. In other words, this prevents people from simply buying "tax shelter" properties and using them for the depreciation write-off, something that was done frequently before the law changed in the 1980s. If you are a "taxpayer in the real property business," on the other hand, you are not a passive investor and the passive loss rule doesn't apply.

Because you will be allowed to take full advantage of the tax advantages, you want to try to get qualified as a "taxpayer in the real property business." To do this, you don't have to be full-time in it, but you have to spend 750 hours a year or about 14 hours a week on your business.

CHAPTER 24

Improving Your Property's Value

You don't necessarily have to spend a great deal of money to improve a property's value, and the strategy of buy, fix, and sell is usually both straight-forward and profitable. Many of the steps below are common sense and inexpensive, but a surprising number of investors neglect these basic items to their own detriment.

LANDSCAPING

The single area that is most often neglected, yet adds the most value for the least amount of money spent, is landscaping. Be cautious in hiring landscape architect firms or you could wind up paying big money here, but don't be afraid to put out a few dollars to dress up your property on your own. Neatly trimmed grass and hedges, a flower garden, some mulch, and a few decorative touches may run you only a few hundred dollars, but a little effort in this regard will significantly increase your property's "curb appeal" as well as overall value.

In my own community, the city has a program that provides annual grants of $125 for street-facing landscape additions. There is no in-come-qualification, and it's available to everyone. You may be lucky enough to own property in a community with a similar program, and you can take advantage of this to help dress up your property.

You can, of course, overdo it. Professional landscaping firms don't come cheap, and they will make a lot of recommendations that might be appropriate for an owner-occupant but aren't cost-effective for an investor. Keep your costs down by doing some of it yourself or by hiring your own gardener to keep the property looking good.

THOROUGH CLEANING

You would be surprised how many properties are shown in a filthy state of disarray. I walked into a vacant house once to look it over for possible purchase, and it smelled so bad of cat urine that I had to hold a cloth over my nose to get through it. I've been in houses on offer that are covered with trash and debris, full of bugs, and with rotten food in the fridge.

OK, the seller blames it on the former tenant, but that's not an excuse. Don't wait to litigate against the former tenant to try to recover damages (which is unlikely). Just clean it up. Showing a house in such a state is unprofessional, and it reflects badly on you as a businessperson. The person viewing the property isn't going to think, "Oh, this investor had really bad tenants." The person is going to think, "Oh, this investor doesn't really care about his properties." And what's more, *you won't get top dollar* for the property simply because you didn't care enough to spend an afternoon cleaning.

Even if the former tenants did leave the property in fairly good condition, you should always give it a thorough, professional cleaning. Ideally, you should bring in professional cleaners and avoid the temptation to just come in for a couple hours with a mop and bucket. There's a big difference between a house that "looks pretty good" and one that is spotless, and it's the spotless one that will sell faster and for bigger money.

$$$ *Part-Time Real Estate Investor Tip* $$$

Don't get caught in the trap of leaving the clean-up to the former tenants, or limiting your own clean-up budget to the amount you can get away with keeping from the former tenant's deposit. Spending a few extra hundred dollars on cleanup can make a difference in sales price of thousands.

DON'T BE AFRAID OF A PROPERTY THAT NEEDS WORK

When you are selling a property, you want it to look as good as possible, but when you are buying one, a different set of rules apply. Those sellers that don't follow the same rules that you do — those that leave trash and debris in their kitchens, don't mow their lawns, and don't bother to clean up the cat smell — aren't going to be selling their properties any time soon, and you can get a better deal. Some sellers won't do this because they don't care or don't have the time, and some may just not have the money or fix-it-up know-how to get the job done. You, on the other hand, do have this know-how and can take advantage of the situation by offering a lower-than-market price for the property.

"Problem properties" don't get sold quickly. Real estate agents don't like to even list them for fear of buyer lawsuits, and those who sell these properties themselves often make the critical mistake of trying to sell it "as is." That's bad for them but good for you. Selling a problem property "as is" is difficult. It takes time, and the seller will almost never get their asking price. *You can capitalize on this situation.* Sellers are often shortsighted when it comes to repairs and renovations and will offer significant discounts for a property that doesn't really need that much work.

GOOD PROBLEMS AND BAD PROBLEMS

Finding a house with "good problems" means finding one with cosmetic and clean-up work needed, which you can do yourself or with unskilled hired labor. The house may look terrible, but if you look beyond that, and consider what you could do to it with a few weeks' worth of work, you'll get the profitable deals. Houses with "bad problems" should usually be avoided. Expensive things that you will need to hire professional contractors for should be avoided. If you have to rewire the entire place, the plumbing is shot, and the roof is sagging in the middle, there's a good chance that the money you spend on renovation will exceed the profit you would make.

Once you've evaluated the property (see the next chapter for information about pre-purchase inspections), go through each problem item and decide if you can fix it yourself and how much each item will cost.

One thing I've discovered is that you can do many home repairs yourself. Although contractors would have you believe that it takes their specialized and expensive knowledge to fix a leaky sink, this is something you can do yourself. It's not rocket science. Stop and think for a moment. You're an intelligent person. Maybe you went to college and have a degree. These contractors are not Harvard Ph.Ds, they're just regular guys, probably with less education than you. *You can do what they do.* A lot of routine repairs and renovations can be done with a little research, a quick search on the internet for information, and a trip to your local home supply store. I've found the clerks at these stores to be knowledgeable enough to tell you what you need to get the job done.

Sometimes my friends are amazed and believe that I am some sort of contracting guru, but this is far from true. My wife recently wanted a new sink in our kitchen. My friends were a bit surprised when I told them I was going to install it myself. The most common reaction I get is, "Oh, do you know how to do that?" Do they think that you have to take a college course in sink installing? Of course, I had never installed a sink before. But "knowing how to do it" is as simple as reading the directions and applying a little common sense. Most people are just afraid to do things like this, and that's why contractors charge so much money. If you are afraid of installing a sink, then you probably shouldn't be in this business. The worst thing that will happen is that you will get wet. Just dive in and give it a try.

A lot of buyers (homeowners and investors alike) make the mistake of being afraid of the term "fixer-upper" when, in reality, most of the time it's the fixer-upper that will yield you the greatest profits. One thing I can't stress enough is that if you are going into this business, you can't be afraid of problems. You just have to recognize them for what they are. There's no such thing as a perfect house. A house with problems is a house with opportunities.

MOLD

Indoor mold is another one of those things that have been blown way out of proportion by greedy lawyers and contractors. Obviously, nobody wants to live in a house that has bathroom walls that are black with mold, but there are two things to realize: (1) almost every house in America has at least a little bit of mold and (2) mold problems can be fixed.

A lot of buyers who don't realize this have a mold inspection done prior to purchase. In almost every case, the mold inspector will find mold and will recommend overpriced measures, and this will become a deal-breaker. Of course, you can use this to your advantage as a negotiating tactic. Telling the seller that there is a mold problem that you will have to attend to will often convince them to lower the price.

Again, turn to the internet and your local home store. You may be able to clean minor mold with commercial solvents. In some cases, you may have to take out some drywall and replace it, but again, this isn't as hard as many people think. If there is a serious mold problem in the bathroom, you can replace the drywall with a mold-resistant drywall that is commonly available at home stores.

The biggest factor in keeping mold under control is controlling moisture. Here are a few tips for preventing mold from occurring or from getting worse:

- Fix leaky plumbing.

- If there is leaking or water damage, dry it, and clean it immediately.

- If mold has penetrated your carpets or ceiling tiles, they will have to be replaced.

- Wash mold off hard surfaces with a good strong detergent and water.

- Make sure the room with the mold problem is ventilated.

- Don't just paint over the moldy areas!

DON'T GO OVERBOARD

There's a difference between renovations you would do on your own home and renovations you would do on an investment home. When working on your own home, your main criteria are your own desires and comfort level. When working on an investment home, your main criteria is profit. Here's an example: In my own home, I'm installing an outdoor koi pond with a waterfall. It may or may not improve the value of the property, but that's secondary. I'm doing it because I like to watch fish and listen to water. This isn't something I would ever do for a rental or investment property for resale.

It's easy to get caught up in the spirit of it. It's fun to take an ugly house and make it pretty. But there are different ways to accomplish that goal. If the kitchen cabinets are worn, you may not need to have the entire set ripped out and replaced. Just putting in new cabinet doors may be adequate.

$$$ *Part-Time Real Estate Investor Tip* $$$

Don't make the mistake of thinking that every dollar you spend on repairs and renovation adds a dollar to the home's resale value. Spending too much on cosmetic repairs can eat too much into your profit!

Above all else, don't blindly follow contractor's recommendations. This is a big mistake that many homeowners and investors make. Because the contractor is a professional, we tend to take them at their word. But remember, they are businesspeople who want to make the most amount of money possible. They will recommend the Cadillac set of renovations when the Ford set would do very well and at half the price.

Also, don't make the mistake of automatically replacing items that don't need to be replaced. If it's old, it's not necessarily bad. Only repair or replace things as needed. Some landlords automatically have the interior of their rentals painted every time a tenant moves out. Granted, sometimes it's necessary, but not always. Look at the condition of the walls. If everything is clean and spotless, the paint is still in good condition, and there's no peeling, why waste the time and money? On the other hand, if the paint is a bit faded, a new paint job is an inexpensive and quick way to make the place look better and increase its value.

CHAPTER 25

Pre-Purchase Inspection

No matter what type of house you are buying—whether it's an immaculate, upscale house in a trendy neighborhood or an "as-is" fixer-upper—you need to do a pre-purchase inspection.

The first thing to address in this chapter is what the inspection is used for. Many buyers use the inspection as an absolute checklist, thinking that if everything on the list is not in perfect order, the deal is off. *That's a big mistake.* There is no such thing as a perfect house. Use the checklist to gather information so you know what you have ahead of you. It will help you understand how much time and money you may have to put into the renovation, and it will also give you leverage in negotiating a better price.

The pre-purchase inspection is especially important because, after you've already made the deal and the property is in your name, it's usually too late to do anything about any problems that come up. There are two ways to go about the inspection, depending on timing. You can do the inspection before you make an offer, although this isn't always possible if you're doing some creative dealing or if you are trying to schedule an outside inspector to do the job for you. Alternately, you can make your offer subject to the property passing inspection. Also, pre-purchase inspections may sometimes be completely impossible, as in the case of a sheriff's sale.

A FEW THINGS TO LOOK FOR

Are there any additions or outbuildings that have been constructed on the property? This may be a good thing, but besides inspecting these additions themselves, find out whether a permit was issued for the construction. If an outbuilding was put up and a permit has not been issued, you may run into some trouble down the road and you may have to tear the structure down, depending on how sticky the local building inspector wants to be.

$$$ *Part-Time Real Estate Investor Tip* $$$

Take a slow drive by the property in the late evening hours. It may seem quiet and peaceful during the day, but it pays to get an idea of what goes on at night in front of a house before buying it. There may be loud noise, gang activity, or drug dealing going on.

Be sure to take a few things with you when you go on your inspection. Besides a checklist, take a flashlight with you so you can inspect poorly lit areas like basements. If you don't (or can't) do a thorough inspection of the roof, at least take a pair of good binoculars with you so you can get a close look at what's up there. A notepad, of course, is essential, and a camera can also be useful for taking pictures of potential problem areas. Take a small pocketknife with you and poke at things like wood beams to check for soft and rotten spots that may be caused by moisture, mold, or termites.

Indoor mold, too, is always something to look out for, but be wary of mold inspectors since almost every home will have at least a small amount of mold present. Look for obvious signs of major mold infections, discolored tile, and dampness in bathrooms and kitchens.

Windows can be a costly replacement item. Even if there is no breakage, they may still have to be replaced. Inspect them closely to see what sort of windows there are—double paned or plain single-pane windows? If you're looking to maintain rental properties and you are going to be paying the heat bills, old-fashioned single pane windows will cost you a bundle in lost energy. Also, check to see if they all open easily. Notice the existence of weather stripping around the windows and doors and whether it is worn and needs to be replaced.

Check the floors. Make it a point to walk around each room, walking heavily or even jumping up and down a time or two, to see if there are any weak spots. Make note of any slanting in the floor. It may be an indication of a foundation problem and could be costly to repair.

Do a quick check of the water pressure. Turn on several water faucets and flush the toilet at the same time, watching the results.

Some investors prefer to do both a personal pre-purchase inspection and a professional, fee-based inspection. Sometimes this can be advantageous. Your first inspection you do yourself, and you take note of any problems or potential problems. Even if you are not sure about the details, take notes even if something just doesn't seem right but you can't put your finger on it. If your pre-purchase inspection reveals a number of problems, making you unsure about purchasing the property, it may well be worthwhile to make your offer with an inspection contingency and then pay a professional inspector to go through the house and follow up on your own findings.

HIRING AN INSPECTOR

If you decide to hire a third party to inspect a property, you should understand right away that not all inspectors are equal, and you should definitely be the one to choose the inspector. You should never let the seller make that selection.

Licensing requirements for home inspectors vary between states, so don't assume that because the inspector has a license that they know what they are doing. Ideally, you should choose an inspector who is not only licensed but has significant experience and may have been in the real estate or contracting business in the past. Your inspector should be knowledgeable about and inspect HVAC, plumbing, electrical, the foundation, and construction. He should provide you a detailed report of all flaws and defects, and you should be allowed to accompany him during the inspection.

You should find an inspector who is impartial. An inspector who is also a contractor may be looking for extra work and may not give you an accurate picture of what is really necessary. Also, the inspector should have no ties to the seller or the real estate agent on the other end of the deal.

Lastly, not all inspectors offer a formal guarantee of their work, but some do.

ESTIMATING THE PROPERTY'S VALUE

The seller's price tag may or may not be anywhere close to what the property is actually worth. Most real estate agents go by "comps," or comparable prices. You can usually determine the cost of recently sold properties in the same neighborhood through tax records or other public records or just by perusing real estate ads. Getting a good idea of what other properties of the same size are selling for in the same area will give you a good idea of whether the selling price is realistic.

Your pre-inspection checklist will also factor in to the calculation. After you have inspected the property, you can make a list of materials you will need to make all necessary repairs and list any other expenses such as contractor fees. If there are $15,000 worth of necessary repairs, which will obviously bring down the sales price, and you have a negotiating tool to ask for (at least) a $15,000 reduction.

$$$ *Part-Time Real Estate Investor Tip* $$$

It's important to gather as much information about a property as possible before closing. That's why pre-purchase inspections are vital. Once the deal is done and you take possession of the property, any major defects that turn up at that time may be your own responsibility. You can, of course, litigate against the seller, but a positive outcome of such litigation is by no means assured.

When researching the tax records to determine prices, be aware that there is a difference between the tax assessed value and the appraised value, and that difference is often significant. It will depend on your local community—but appraised value will often be much higher than the tax assessment.

SELLER DISCLOSURES

Your first strategy is to conduct your own inspection, but seller disclosures can also be useful if you don't rely on them alone. Use this information only as a "secondary" detail, and realize that a seller is required only to disclose problems they know about and that seller disclosure doesn't mean the seller is giving you a warranty against the present or future condition of the property. If the seller states that they are unaware of any problems with the roof and the following winter it collapses, you probably don't have much recourse. The seller disclosure is a guideline only and should not be taken as absolute fact.

Laws vary between states, but most sellers must complete a disclosure statement, and this lists all known problems and defects. Even if your state doesn't require this, you can still ask the sellers to fill out a disclosure form, and most will comply.

INVESTIGATE INTANGIBLES

There are a great many things to look out for when examining a property for purchase, but the initial walk-through to look for cosmetic and structural problems isn't the end of it. You can easily fix the leaky faucet in about 15 minutes, but there are also some intangible things that you want to consider before making an offer.

- First, you must become knowledgeable about the title. Are there title problems ("clouded" title) and are there multiple second mortgages? Regardless of how you are purchasing the property (land contract, "subject to," or conventional mortgage), a fuzzy title can cause big problems down the road.

That's not to say that title problems should be a deal killer, but you should be aware of them, know what to expect, what the potential problems may be, and how you can fix them.

- What about the neighborhood? The house may be in perfect shape, but do the neighbors have loud backyard parties every Saturday? You'll have a hard time keeping good tenants if you're renting the property. Take a walk through the neighborhood and try to strike up a conversation with people you see outside. Ask them frankly about the neighbors and whether they have ever had any problems or complaints.

- What is the house's history? Again, it may be in perfect shape now, but does the house have a bad reputation? Did it used to be a drug house or a center of criminal activity? Do people say that it's haunted? Was somebody murdered in the house? These sorts of things can also have a big impact on a property's resale value.

INSPECTION CHECKLIST

Address: _____

Agent contact information: _____

Seller contact information: _____

Sale price: _____

Check the following items. Make notes as to condition, and rate on a scale of one to five, with five being excellent and one being poor.

Exterior:

	Rating	Notes
Foundation	_____	_____
Paint	_____	_____
Siding	_____	_____
Windows	_____	_____
Screens	_____	_____
Outbuildings	_____	_____
Porch	_____	_____
Deck	_____	_____
Steps	_____	_____
Roof	_____	_____
Driveway	_____	_____
Fencing	_____	_____
Gutters/downpipes	_____	_____
Landscaping	_____	_____
Location	_____	_____

Kitchen:

Tile/wall _____ _____

Appliances _____ _____

Floor _____ _____

Cabinets _____ _____

Sink/plumbing _____ _____

Mold _____ _____

Bathrooms:

Toilet _____ _____

Tub/shower _____ _____

Sink _____ _____
Mold _____ _____

Electric _____ _____

Ventilation _____ _____

Other details:

Number of bedrooms _____ _____

Carpet _____ _____

Electrical outlets _____ _____

Living area _____ _____

Extra rooms _____ _____

Storage _____ _____

Lot size _____ _____

CHAPTER 26

More Is Better:
Snowballing Your Real Estate Investments

It's addicting. One piece of real estate will make you a little money, so a dozen will make you more. Theoretically, at least.

Buying one or two pieces of property and making them into a rental may yield you $100 a week of net profit. Now when you explain to your friends and relatives that you're getting $100 a week in return for very little effort, they will get excited, offer praise, and say how wonderful it is to have a few hundred dollars extra. But you're not in business to get enough money to go out to dinner a couple times a week and buy a few tanks of gas. You're in business to get rich.

The same thing happened to me after I started a dot-com business. Because I was spending virtually no time on maintaining the business, my friends got excited and told me how wonderful it was to have "extra" money. I balked right away though, complaining that it wasn't enough and I wanted more. They didn't understand it, but they were seeing my $100 a week as "extra," and I was seeing it as part of my regular income. If you're in business, whether it's real estate or a dot-com, there is no "extra" income. It's all just income that goes to the bottom line. Don't look at your real estate profits as "extra." Looking at it that way will put you in a complacent mood. Although we can't complain about contentment, we do complain about not having enough money. If you are happy with $100 a week, you're not going to work very hard to get to $1,000 a week.

LEVERAGE YOUR INVESTMENT

Beginning investors make the mistake of thinking that because they are not yet wealthy, they will be unable to buy more than one or two properties. This is a fallacy that will trap you into working your real estate business for small change instead of big money.

Let's say, for the sake of round figures, that the average investment property in your area costs $100,000 and that you will be able to purchase said properties with an average of $10,000 to cover down payment, closing costs, and repairs. Your goal is to have a million dollars' worth of properties, which in this case, would be ten houses. You have only $10,000 in cash though, so you think you can only buy one house.

But consider this: Suppose you use that $10,000 to buy a house that you rent out, and after a year's time it increases in value. The increased value plus your rental profits could realistically give you an extra $10,000 after 12 months. And so, after a year's time, you take out a loan against the increased equity you have in the property, combine it with your profits, and you buy another house. Now you have two. It would be a very easy matter to double your property every year, just by leveraging the increased equity you have gained through the combination of principal payments you have made and the increased value of the home that accrues over time. So after two years, you have four homes, and after three years, you have eight. Some time early in your fourth year, you reach ten houses, and you hit that million-dollar goal. And you put out a total of $10,000 worth of your own cash. Everything after that came from increased equity and profits. Let's draw it out:

You buy your first $300,000 property with $60,000 down, leaving you with a $240,000 mortgage. Let's assume 4 percent, which would give you payments of roughly $1,540 principal and interest. Add on taxes and insurance and it may bring it up to roughly $1,900. You rent the property out at $2,100, for a $200 a month net profit. Let's also assume that real estate appreciates in your area at about 7 percent annually. After the first year, you have made the following:

Rental profits, 12 months @ $200	$2,400
Principal contributions for 12 months	4,200
Appreciation	21,000
Total	27,600

You take that money and buy a second house. In your second year, you still earn $2,400 in rents from your first house, but it also yields you $4,400 in principal contributions this year, and also because the appreciation is compounding, your property is now worth $343,470. And we're not even taking into account the tax advantages you are going to enjoy. Of course, it's all theoretical and approximate, but you can see where this is going. Of course, your results may differ, depending on how much property appreciates in your town and what the going rates for rentals may be. A second thing to consider is that after the first year, your appreciation will probably be greater, because you will be fixing up the property. But every year, each property increases in value, and that increased value can be used to purchase additional properties. In this way, you can use your initial investment to leverage a million dollars' worth of property in just five years.

The first year or so may seem slow. It may seem like it's not worthwhile, because you're just getting that small amount of cash flow from your one rental. But remember, it builds up quickly, and after you have created a head of steam, that little trickle of profits turns into a downpour.

Some investors, brokers, and especially bankers (whom you should almost never listen to) will give you a lot of figures and formulas for real estate investing, and for the most part, these are useless. One thing the bankers are especially fond of is figuring net return on investment (ROI) for a property, and they arrive at this ratio by dividing the net income you receive by the purchase price. However, this is a false ratio that in reality is quite deceiving. The only way this is relevant is if you pay cash outright for a property. For example, a banker will figure that you receive a net income of $5,000 a year on a property that is worth $100,000 and say that you have a 5 percent return. But how much actual cash did you lay out to get that $100,000 property? If you paid 10 percent down, you spent $10,000 of actual cash to acquire the property. The true ratio that is more relevant should be the net income divided by the amount of cash used for acquisition. In this case, that figure indicates that you do not have a 5 percent return. You have a 50 percent return.

$$$ *Part-Time Real Estate Investor Tip* $$$

Don't neglect the value of the equity that gradually accrues in your property. Even if you only break even for the first couple of years, you're not really just breaking even because you are reducing your mortgage debt and increasing your assets, which you can leverage later to purchase additional properties. In other words, if you break even your first year, but the principal portion of your payments amount to $2,000, then although you don't see it in actual cash, you have really made $2,000.

ALWAYS BE OPEN TO NEW DEALS

People who are too hesitant to take advantage of a deal usually wind up with less property to call their own and a lower income, while paying more for everything. You certainly don't want to jump the gun and not think things out—we've all known people who think things to death, haven't we? Maybe that was you in the past. You overanalyzed a situation: a purchase, a relationship, whatever, and in so doing, made the decision too late.

When you start your real estate business or any business for that matter, you will have a certain set of operating rules in place by necessity, but those rules should not be held so hard and fast that you cheat yourself out of an opportunity. Suppose, for example, that you decide that you are going to buy one property a year. That's a good strategy. But midway through the year, just a few months after you purchased your most recent property, you get wind of a deal. A homeowner is in trouble with the bank and has a home that needs a little cosmetic repair. The homeowner has some equity in the home but is several payments behind and just can't catch up. What's more, the owner, realizing that the home is in need of some fixing up, is willing to just walk away from it. You could possibly get it on a "subject to" deal just by paying the back payments. You do a little research and find out that the neighborhood is a good rental neighborhood, and you could rent it out at a good profit. What do you do?

You could stay steadfast to your strategy and pass on the deal, dig in your heels, and say, "I've made a rule and I'm sticking to it." A lot of people do that. But you have the cash to make the deal. A little further research shows that just a little bit of fix-up would yield you instant equity in the property. So you take the plunge, fix it up, and either rent it out and achieve positive cash flow or sell it at a substantial profit. You broke your rules, but you ended up with more money.

Don't be afraid to break your own rules.

WHEN IS THE RIGHT TIME TO START?

When is the best time to get started in real estate? Is there a formula? Should you wait until you have a certain amount of money in the bank, wait until the kids are finished with college, or wait until you pay off some debts? Wait until you retire? Until the economy improves? Until the Federal Reserve lowers the interest rate? The answer is, do it *right now*. Even if you are broke, in debt, your wife is getting ready to leave you, your dog ran away, your roof needs to be fixed, and there are personal and financial situations that are getting in the way. *Do it right now.*

Now, you will no doubt run to your banker or financial advisor and that individual will tell you a different story. They will tell you to wait, to be conservative and prudent, and they will give you a long list of things to do before you take your first step. Whatever you do, don't listen to these people.

Yes, there is risk involved, and you will want to do whatever you can to keep those risks at a minimum by starting out part-time. "Don't quit your day job." That comes later. The best way to start a real estate business is to start out part-time with one or two properties while you still have another income from a job or other business. Your first couple of properties will make you a little money, emphasis on the "little." The real wealth builds up over the course of years. A more reasonable goal would be to quit your day job in five years.

CHAPTER 27

Getting in Over Your Head

In the last chapter, we talked about the most appropriate time to get started in the real estate business. The right time to get started is always "right now." But let's consider how fast you should proceed.

I knew one investor (who caused me no end of headache) who decided she wanted to be a big-time real estate tycoon. Instead of trying to build up her empire gradually, she took all her money and some of her husband's and quickly bought as many properties as she could get her hands on. Because her husband had a successful business, she was able to get mortgages for the properties, but she made a critical mistake. Her philosophy was that breaking even on cash flow was acceptable because later on down the road (many years later on down the road) she would have equity.

This sort of break-even mentality is a surefire way to quick disaster. If you are breaking even on your properties, it's true that you are actually coming out ahead, because you are building equity and getting some tax advantages. But what about your cash flow? If you're breaking even, you have none. Now consider that if you have 20 or 30 properties and you are renting them out or selling them on land contract, and taking in about as much as you are paying out, there will come a time when one or more of your properties are vacant. In the case of my acquaintance, at any given time, two or three of her properties were vacant, and at least half of them were delinquent in paying. She wasn't able to make up the difference out of pocket, went into default, and lost every single one of them.

And so we see that breaking even isn't always breaking even. When you calculate a break-even figure on paper, it assumes that the property is "performing" or is being rented out or sold on land contract. Beginning investors may neglect to factor in a vacancy rate—and if you're only breaking even, if your property is vacant for even a single month, you are losing money. Before you set prices, try to figure out an approximate vacancy rate to figure into the calculation. This isn't always easy to come up with, and in any case, it's nothing but a guess, but it's better than nothing. Check out the area, talk to other landlords and property managers, and take your best shot. If you have a rental property by the university for example, you will probably have a high turnover and will want to factor in a high vacancy rate. A student property might realistically be vacant for two months out of the year. Factor this in when setting your price. For example: Suppose your expenses are $1,000 a month for a unit. This comes to $12,000 a year. If you anticipate that your unit will be rented for only 10 out of 12 months, divide that $12,000 by 10 (the number of months it will be generating revenue), and your break-even rent will be $1,200 a month.

That's not to say that a break-even strategy is always bad. If you have one or two properties that you are breaking even on, and you have a source of extra money from another business that can subsidize any temporary losses, then in the long run you will still come out ahead. But if you're just breaking even, you have to be able to plan for a temporary loss, and have enough resources to cover that loss. If, for example, you don't have a lot of resources, are going into the real estate business with very little money, and your day job just gives you enough to get by, what will happen when your unit becomes vacant for two months? If you can't pay the $750 a month in expenses for that time, you're going to get into some serious trouble, and may lose your property.

It is certainly possible to get into real estate with no money, and it's a great way to build wealth. But proceed with caution and plan for losses ahead of time. As I said before, real estate empires that are built too quickly with no money have a tendency to collapse like houses of cards.

THE PART-TIME STRATEGY

It sounds great to build up a real estate business in your spare time, and in fact, it's the safest strategy to do so. The catch is, you need another source of income for your first few years of real estate wheeling and dealing. That's the big mistake my acquaintance made: She was trying to leverage a small amount of wealth to buy dozens of properties all at once without any other source of income.

Yes, we all want to become millionaires overnight, but it doesn't happen that often in real life. It can happen in a five to 10 years. Take advantage of every opportunity to be sure, but don't be in too much of a hurry and don't over-extend yourself. Try to build positive cash flow. Once you have built your business up enough to the point where you can give yourself a sustainable paycheck every week, then feel free to quit that day job and go full-time.

Will there be a housing crash?

One thing that beginning investors are afraid of is a housing crash. They are afraid that they will buy property, its value will decrease, and they will not be able to sustain their business and will find themselves in over their heads.

This is certainly a concern, but not a big one. For the most part, real estate is one of the safest investments there is, and there's no reason why, if you pursue an aggressive but sane strategy, this should be a concern to you. Home values rise steadily over time, and it's a pretty safe bet that if you buy a home today, it will be worth a lot more in 10 years. In recent years, home prices on average throughout the United States rose more than 10 percent per year, with some regions rising substantially more than that.

Here's some interesting and enlightening statistics. In 1968, the median price of a home in the United States was $20,100. By 1998, 30 years later, the median was $128,400—about a 630 percent increase. Between 1968 and 2004, the average price increase has been 6.4 percent a year. In some years, the increase averaged in the double digits, while the lowest increase was in 1989, when it increased less than 1 percent. Nonetheless, there was not a single year in that 36-year span where there was a decrease in the median price. In 2005, low interest rates and a strong economy pushed growth up, and home prices rose an average of 13.6 percent; and out of

149 metro areas listed, 67 of them had double-digit percent gains. Even in my area, South Bend, Indiana, prices increased 8.8 percent, a good increase, given that South Bend is not a wealthy town. The market remained strong, peaking in 2006, but then came a massive correction, one that loosely coincided with the so-called Great Recession of 2008-2009. April 2007 saw a nearly 11 percent year-over-year decline in the median price of residential homes, the biggest decline since 1970, according to the U.S. Department of Commerce. Once the recession ended, the real estate industry began a recovery that started slow but gathered greater force with every passing year, more than making up for previous losses. And that has left us where are now, strong markets that have some people wondering if home prices must inevitably decline.

You may be somewhat concerned about how interest rates affect housing prices. Interest rates were at an all-time low for a long time, and they may be on the way up. This does affect your business—but pay attention here— *it doesn't mean that you shouldn't be in this business.* In fact, housing prices continue to rise throughout the world, not just in the United States. And if you look at history, whenever the interest rates rise, what happens is that housing prices increase at a slower pace. They do not drop.

CHAPTER 28

Tips and Techniques

There is a lot to learn about real estate investing, but the best way to learn is by diving right in. You will make mistakes, and you will lose money on some deals, but you will learn more along the way, and you will build wealth in the end.

One of the greatest sources of wisdom is other real estate investors and professionals. You can, of course, buy and read dozens of books, take courses, and become certified and licensed, but there's nothing like picking the brain of somebody who's already made their million.

Try to seek out and meet people who have become successful in real estate. Take them out to lunch and be honest and up-front, tell them that you want to get into the business and want their advice and insight. Most of the time, they will be happy to give it to you, and you will learn a great deal in the process. In this chapter, I'm including a few more pearls of wisdom I have picked up along the way from some of the most successful and wealthy investors I've met.

AGENT PROSPECTING AND FSBOS

Real estate agents are always on the lookout for new business, and one way they find it is to prospect FSBOs ("for sale by owner"). They will try to convince the seller that they should abandon their FSBO strategy and list their property with them. They will argue endlessly about the troubles the FSBO seller will have, how difficult the process is, and how they can get them a better deal. In some cases, the agents tend to be a little pompous believing that they are the only ones who should be allowed to sell a house, and that anyone who tries to sell a house on their own is a fool. If any agent tries these tactics with you, *send them packing immediately.*

There is some validity in their argument *if you are an individual who is selling a single property*. It's true, it's a lot of work to sell a house, and if you're not dedicated to the process or don't have the time, the agent can probably do a better job. But remember, you're in a different boat than most FSBO sellers. You're not just selling a single property. You are a real estate investor, and this is your job. You are just as much of a professional as the real estate agent. You aren't just trying to unload a piece of property. You are trying to turn a profit, and that agent's 6 percent commission will eat into your profit. Wouldn't you rather put in the hours and keep that 6 percent yourself?

WORK WITH THE MONEY PEOPLE

If you're in the business of buying and selling real estate, you're really in two businesses: real estate and finance. Most people just don't have the resources to pay cash for a house. They have to go to a third party, such as a bank or a mortgage broker, to borrow the money. You, as the real estate investor, want to make it as easy as possible for people to buy your properties. The best way to do this is to have connections in the financial services industry.

If done right, it works wonderfully, but there is a potential downside to this strategy. Here's an example. I had an acquaintance who purchased several properties for flipping (buy, renovate, sell). He sold them on "FSBO/owner finance" terms, which is usually a good tactic. He worked with a mortgage broker who vetted each deal before he would close. The reasoning was that he would sell on a land contract with a three-year balloon payment, and then after the three-year term was up, the broker agreed to find financing for the buyer. Ideally, this would be good. Too often, people buy on owner-financing terms (which almost always carries a balloon) but then have no idea what they will do when the balloon payment comes due. If that balloon payment comes due in two or three years, that may not be enough time for someone to clean up their credit and save up enough for a sizeable down payment. Having it all pre-arranged ahead of time takes a little bit of the worry out of the transaction for both sides.

But here's the trouble: Mortgage brokers tend to be conservative and tend to want buyers to qualify just as if they were applying for a bank loan. The problem here is that in almost every case, people buy "owner-financing" homes because they cannot qualify for a bank loan. That's why you can get a higher price for your property, and you can charge higher-than-normal interest. In the case of my acquaintance, the mortgage broker killed off many deals including one with me. But I had the last laugh—a year later, I drove by the house I had been interested in, and the "for sale by owner" sign was still in the front yard.

With that caveat in mind, working with a funding source or mortgage broker can be an excellent strategy. The best approach is to work with only one to create a tighter relationship, a little loyalty, and more leverage with the financial professional. Some real estate people simply gather the information from their buyers and send it out to dozens of brokers every time, and they usually wind up spending time and still not getting the best deal for their buyers. If you work with only one, that individual will get to know you, know how you work, and what types of deals you are likely to bring to the table. The deals will go through faster, because the broker will understand ahead of time what needs to be done. And what's more important, the broker will understand that you have an exclusive relationship, and if he puts the time into making a quote and arranging a deal, he will benefit. The problem with sending out the deal to several brokers at once is that each broker will have no assurance that they will gain anything for all their hard work.

THE BALLOON PAYMENT

This is an important part of the owner-financing deal. It simply takes a 30-year private mortgage and includes a clause in the contract that makes the contract due in full at a certain time. Most owner-financing deals carry this clause, although you certainly don't have to. If you just want to have a steady income every month for the next 30 years, just carry the contract yourself with no balloon.

The period of time after which the note comes due (balloon clause) varies. There are some less scrupulous real estate investors who offer easy owner-financing but then include a one-year balloon clause in the contract. The problem here is that one of the main reasons for the balloon is to allow the buyer to build up equity and clean up their credit. Remember, almost every person you sell to on owner-finance terms is going to be credit-challenged. One year is just not enough time to reach a good credit status. The buyer will build up very little equity. The unscrupulous seller enforces the one-year balloon, knowing full well ahead of time that the buyer is unlikely to be able to obtain third party financing. The seller forecloses, and the buyer loses their down payment and whatever equity they put into the property. The seller is just using the balloon clause as a way of getting a lot more cash flow than would otherwise be possible with a straight rental, since they will usually charge a down payment significantly more than a rental deposit.

A more realistic approach would be to offer a contract with a five-year bal-loon clause. Five years is ample time for a buyer to clean up credit prob-lems, and after five years, the buyer will have built up some equity that can be used as leverage to obtain third party financing. In this way, you can have cash flow for five years, and after that time, you can cash out of your property when the buyer gets third party financing.

Also, remember that a funding source will take into account how long a contract has been in force. A funding source is very likely to offer financing to a buyer who has been making timely payments on a property for five years than they would for one who has been paying for just one year.

BUYING AND SELLING LAND CONTRACTS

Another option is to sell your land contract to a third party. A private mortgage or land contract is a negotiable document that can be bought and sold, just like conventional mortgages are bought and sold between financial institutions. If you are carrying a mortgage for a buyer, you own a document that you can sell at a discount to another investor. There are investors who specialize in buying private mortgages like this. Again, keep scrupulous records of payments. If you have a seasoned land contract and a buyer who has been making timely payments for at least three to five years, you can probably sell your contract to an investor. The investor will give you a lump-sum cash payment and then make his profit by collecting the payments over time. There will be a discount involved. For example, if there is $50,000 still owing on the contract, the investor may offer you $40,000 cash. The investor then earns money two ways: first by buying a $50,000 contract for $40,000, and second, by continuing to collect pay-ments with interest over time from the buyer.

Depending on your circumstances, you don't even need to sell 100 percent of the contract. If you have a $50,000 contract, but don't want to let the whole thing go but still have an immediate need for some cash, you can sell part of the note.

If you have cash, as an investor, you can get involved in the other end of this deal and buy other investors' notes yourself. When you are buying notes, the discount will depend on the quality of the deal. There are some investors who specialize in buying delinquent notes. If your buyer has been consistently past due in payments or is even a few months behind, there are still people who may be willing to buy the note — but the catch is, they will buy it at a much deeper discount. The result is a good deal for the buyer of the note, since they get an asset and the possibility of foreclosing on a property for significantly less than market value. When you buy a delinquent note like this, you earn the right to collect not only the current payments, but also the delinquent ones.

FINDING MONEY: PARTNERS VERSUS INVESTORS

There are some deals where you can arrange to acquire a property for little or nothing down, but there are other deals where you are going to need cash, and lots of it. If you don't have it, you have a dilemma. But cash deals are not necessarily closed to you just because you don't have the cash.

There are two ways to obtain cash for a deal: Take on a partner or borrow it from an investor. There are advantages to each, but in most cases, you will be better off not taking partners, but instead obtaining financing. Financing is hard to come by, however, and the only financing sources may be hard money lenders who charge very high rates of interest.

Nonetheless, you will usually come out ahead even if you have to pay a hard money lender a significant amount of interest. It's better, for example, to pay a hard money lender 18 percent, plus points, than to split your profit 50-50 with a partner. It's not always immediately clear, but you will find that this is almost always the case. It's our natural tendency to shy away from high-interest lenders, but they can be your best friend.

Let's work the numbers. Suppose you buy a fixer-upper for $150,000 and expect that you will have to put $20,000 into renovations. Afterwards, you anticipate selling the property for $200,000. Now if you have all that cash yourself, you lay out the $200,000, and take the $50,000 as profit. But, if you're not that lucky, you offer a partner a deal: You pay the money, I do the work, and we split the profits. In this case, you get $25,000 at the end of the deal. But suppose you find a hard money lender or private investor who will charge you three points, plus 18 percent interest. You expect that it will take you about six months to renovate and resell, so the total cost to the hard money lender will be $5,100 (points) plus $30,600 interest, for a total of $35,700. Subtract that from the $50,000, and your profit at the end of the deal is $14,300.

$$$ *Part-Time Real Estate Investor Tip* $$$

One of the most famous cynical lines ever uttered was by Woody Allen, who said, "90 percent of success is just showing up." And Woody had the right dope on that one. Much of your success as a real estate investor will simply depend on being there. Being in the right place at the right time. Just being the one who has the foresight to be present around deals that are being made.

Conclusion

Having read this book, you will have gained some insight into how this business works; and hopefully, you will realize one thing above all else: Real estate investing isn't just for the rich. While having cash (either your own or somebody else's) will always give you an edge, there are deals that can be made with little or no money. You can get started right now. There's no need to wait until you have a "war chest" of money. No matter what your situation is, today is the day for you to get started on your real estate business. Instead of waiting until you have more money in the bank, why not get started right away and work on getting that money in the bank with a few preliminary real estate deals? Once you have the money in the bank, you will be able to make more deals and increase it even more.

THE TOP 10 RULES

There's a lot to remember, but there are 10 basic rules to becoming a part-time real estate investor making huge profits, and I'm presenting them here:

1. *Be unconventional.* If you limit yourself to conventional loans and mainstream deals, you may never get your business of the ground. Don't be afraid to be creative or to offer something unusual or even outrageous. Don't be afraid to go outside of the standard banker/ real estate agent protocol.

2. *You don't need money to get started.* There are always deals to be had for little or no money down. Don't be afraid to seek them out and start your business today.

3. *Don't limit yourself to no-money-down deals.* If you must start with no-money-down deals, do so, but once you have built up some capital and equity, take advantage of it to open yourself up to more deals.

4. *Be persistent.* Especially if you are making creative offers, you won't be able to close every deal. Some people will say "no" to you, so get used to it, move on to the next one, and keep asking until you find someone who will say "yes."

5. *Don't go too fast.* You can start today with nothing, but avoid the temptation to take on dozens of highly leveraged deals in a short period of time. Beware of "get rich quick" real estate seminars. If you get in over your head and operate too close to the margin, you could lose everything very quickly.

6. *Buy your own house first.* If you're not a homeowner yourself before you start buying and selling, become one.

7. *Understand renovation.* Besides gaining a basic understanding of how to install a sink, understand how to spot exactly what a house needs to have done to it before you can resell it and how much it will cost you. Conduct a thorough pre-purchase inspection before making an offer.

8. *Increase curb appeal with simple things.* You can make a house more saleable and at a higher price with simple, inexpensive things like landscaping, a neat lawn, and a good paint job.

9. *Free yourself from the illusion of security.* When you realize that there is no such thing as security, whether it's from a job or from working for yourself, you will be free to be creative, to try new things, and to pursue your goals. Not everything you try will work, but some of them will, and that's what makes the process worthwhile.

10. And realize this: A millionaire is somebody just like you who just happens to have a lot of money. There's nothing special about a millionaire, nothing magical, and nothing secret, and there's no reason in the world that you can't be one too.

Glossary

401(k)/403(b) An investment plan sponsored by an employer that enables individuals to set aside pre-tax income for retirement or emergency purposes. 401(k) plans are provided by private corporations. 403(b) plans are provided by non-profit organizations.

401(k)/403(b) Loan A type of financing using a loan against the money accumulated in a 401(k)/403(b) plan.

Abatement Sometimes referred to as free rent or early occupancy. A condition that could happen in addition to the primary term of the lease.

Above Building Standard Finishes and specialized designs that have been upgraded in order to accommodate a tenant's requirements.

Absorption Rate The speed and amount of time at which rentable space, in square feet, is filled.

Abstract or Title Search The process of reviewing all transactions that have been recorded publicly in order to determine whether any defects in the title exist that could interfere with a clear property ownership transfer.

Accelerated Cost Recovery System A calculation for taxes to provide more depreciation for the first few years of ownership.

Accelerated Depreciation A method of depreciation where the value of a property depreciates faster in the first few years after purchasing it.

Acceleration Clause A clause in a contract that gives the lender the right to demand immediate payment of the balance of the loan if the borrower defaults on the loan.

Acceptance The seller's written approval of a buyer's offer.

Ad Valorem A Latin phrase that translates as "according to value". Refers to a tax that is imposed on a property's value that is typically based on the local government's evaluation of the property.

Addendum An addition or update for an existing contract between parties.

Additional Principal Payment Additional money paid to the lender, apart from the scheduled loan payments, to pay more of the principal balance, shortening the length of the loan.

Adjustable-Rate Mortgage (ARM) A home loan with an interest rate that is adjusted periodically in order to reflect changes in a specific financial resource.

Adjusted Funds From Operations (AFFO) The rate of REIT performance or ability to pay dividends that is used by many analysts who have concerns about the quality of earnings as measured by Funds From Operations (FFO).

Adjustment Date The date at which the interest rate is adjusted for an adjustable-rate mortgage (ARM).

Adjustment Period The amount of time between adjustments for an interest rate in an ARM.

Administrative Fee A percentage of the value of the assets under management, or a fixed annual dollar amount charged to manage an account.

Advances The payments the servicer makes when the borrower fails to send a payment.

Adviser A broker or investment banker who represents an owner in a transaction and is paid a retainer and/or a performance fee once a financing or sales transaction has closed.

Agency Closing A type of closing in which a lender uses a title company or other firm as an agent to finish a loan.

Agency Disclosure A requirement in most states that agents who act for both buyers or sellers must disclose who they are working for in the transaction.

Aggregation Risk The risk that is associated with warehousing mortgages during the process of pooling them for future security.

Agreement of Sale A legal document the buyer and seller must approve and sign that details the price and terms in the transaction.

Alienation Clause The provision in a loan that requires the borrower to pay the total balance of the loan at once if the property is sold or the ownership transferred.

Alternative Mortgage A home loan that does not match the standard terms of a fixed-rate mortgage.

Alternative or Specialty Investments Types of property that are not considered to be conventional real estate investments, such as self-storage facilities, mobile homes, timber, agriculture, or parking lots.

Amortization The usual process of paying a loan's interest and principal via scheduled monthly payments.

Amortization Schedule Chart or table that shows the percentage of each payment that will be applied toward principal and interest over the life of the mortgage and how the loan balance decreases until it reaches zero.

Amortization Tables The mathematical tables that are used to calculate what a borrower's monthly payment will be.

Amortization Term The number of months it will take to amortize the loan.

Anchor The business or individual who is serving as the primary draw to a commercial property.

Annual Mortgagor Statement A yearly statement to borrowers which details the remaining principal balance and amounts paid throughout the year for taxes and interest.

Annual Percentage Rate (APR) The interest rate that states the actual cost of borrowing money over the course of a year.

Annuity The regular payments of a fixed sum.

Application The form a borrower must complete in order to apply for a mortgage loan, including information such as income, savings, assets, and debts.

Application Fee A fee some lenders charge that may include charges for items such as property appraisal or a credit report unless those fees are included elsewhere.

Appraisal The estimate of the value of a property on a particular date given by a professional appraiser, usually presented in a written document.

Appraisal Fee The fee charged by a professional appraiser for his estimate of the market value of a property.

Appraisal Report The written report presented by an appraiser regarding the value of a property.

Appraised Value The dollar amount a professional appraiser assigned to the value of a property in his report.

Appraiser A certified individual who is qualified by education, training, and experience to estimate the value of real and personal property.

Appreciation An increase in the home's or property's value.

Appreciation Return The amount gained when the value of the real estate assets increases during the current quarter.

Arbitrage The act of buying securities in one market and selling them immediately in another market in order to profit from the difference in price.

ARM Index A number that is publicly published and used as the basis for interest rate adjustments on an ARM.

As-Is Condition A phrase in a purchase or lease contract in which the new tenant accepts the existing condition of the premises as well as any physical defects.

Assessed Value The value placed on a home that is determined by a tax assessor in order to calculate a tax base.

Assessment (1) The approximate value of a property. (2) A fee charged in addition to taxes in order to help pay for items such as water, sewer, street improvements, etc.

Assessor A public officer who estimates the value of a property for the purpose of taxation.

Asset A property or item of value owned by an individual or company.

Asset Management Fee A fee that is charged to investors based on the amount of money they have invested into real estate assets for the particular fund or account.

Asset Management The various tasks and areas around managing real estate assets from the initial investment until the time it is sold.

Asset Turnover The rate of total revenues for the previous 12 months divided by the average total assets.

Assets Under Management The amount of the current market value of real estate assets that a manager is responsible to manage and invest.

Assignee Name The individual or business to whom the lease, mortgage, or other contract has been re-assigned.

Assignment The transfer of rights and responsibilities from one party to another for paying a debt. The original party remains liable for the debt should the second party default.

Assignor The person who transfers the rights and interests of a property to another.

Assumable Mortgage A mortgage that is capable of being transferred to a different borrower.

Assumption The act of assuming the mortgage of the seller.

Assumption Clause A contractual provision that enables the buyer to take responsibility for the mortgage loan from the seller.

Assumption Fee A fee charged to the buyer for processing new records when they are assuming an existing loan.

Attorn To agree to recognize a new owner of a property and to pay rent to the new landlord.

Average Common Equity The sum of the common equity for the last five quarters divided by five.

Average Downtime The number of months that are expected between a lease's expiration and the beginning of a replacement lease under the current market conditions.

Average Free Rent The number of months the rent abatement concession is expected to be granted to a tenant as part of an incentive to lease under current market conditions.

Average Occupancy The average rate of each of the previous 12 months that a property was occupied.

Average Total Assets The sum of the total assets of a company for the previous five quarters divided by five.

Back Title Letter A letter that an attorney receives from a title insurance company before examining the title for insurance purposes.

Back-End Ratio The calculation lenders use to compare a borrower's gross monthly income to their total debt.

Balance Sheet A statement that lists an individual's assets, liabilities, and net worth.

Balloon Loan A type of mortgage in which the monthly payments are not large enough to repay the loan by the end of the term, and the final payment is one large payment of the remaining balance.

Balloon Payment The final huge payment due at the end of a balloon mortgage.

Balloon Risk The risk that a borrower may not be able to come up with the funds for the balloon payment at maturity.

Bankrupt The state an individual or business is in if they are unable to repay their debt when it is due.

Bankruptcy A legal proceeding where a debtor can obtain relief from payment of certain obligations through restructuring their finances.

Base Loan Amount The amount that forms the basis for the loan payments.

Base Principal Balance The original loan amount once adjustments for subsequent fundings and principal payments have been made without including accrued interest or other unpaid debts.

Base Rent A certain amount that is used as a minimum rent, providing for rent increases over the term of the lease agreement.

Base Year The sum of actual taxes and operating expenses during a given year, often that in which a lease begins.

Basis Point A term for 1/100 of one percentage point.

Before-Tax Income An individual's income before taxes have been deducted.

Below-Grade Any structure or part of a structure that is below the surface of the ground that surrounds it.

Beneficiary An employee who is covered by the benefit plan his or her company provides.

Beta The measurement of common stock price volatility for a company in comparison to the market.

Bid The price or range an investor is willing to spend on whole loans or securities.

Bill of Sale A written legal document that transfers the ownership of personal property to another party.

Binder (1) A report describing the conditions of a property's title. (2) An early agreement between seller and buyer.

Biweekly Mortgage A mortgage repayment plan that requires payments every two weeks to help repay the loan over a shorter amount of time.

Blanket Mortgage A rare type of mortgage that covers more than one of the borrower's properties.

Blind Pool A mixed fund that accepts capital from investors without specifying property assets.

Bond Market The daily buying and selling of thirty-year treasury bonds that also affects fixed rate mortgages.

Book Value The value of a property based on its purchase amount plus upgrades or other additions with depreciation subtracted.

Break-Even Point The point at which a landlord's income from rent matches expenses and debt.

Bridge Loan A short-term loan for individuals or companies that are still seeking more permanent financing.

Broker A person who serves as a go-between for a buyer and seller.

Brokerage The process of bringing two or more parties together in exchange for a fee, commission, or other compensation.

Buildable Acres The portion of land that can be built on after allowances for roads, setbacks, anticipated open spaces, and unsuitable areas have been made.

Building Code The laws set forth by the local government regarding end use of a given piece of property. These law codes may dictate the design, materials used, and/or types of improvements that will be allowed.

Building Standard Plus Allowance A detailed list provided by the landlord stating the standard building materials and costs necessary to make the premises inhabitable.

Build-Out Improvements to a property's space that have been implemented according to the tenant's specifications.

Build-to-Suit A way of leasing property, usually for commercial purposes, in which the developer or landlord builds to a tenant's specifications.

Buydown A term that usually refers to a fixed-rate mortgage for which additional payments can be applied to the interest rate for a temporary period, lowering payments for a period of one to three years.

Buydown Mortgage A style of home loan in which the lender receives a higher payment in order to convince them to reduce the interest rate during the initial years of the mortgage.

Buyer's Remorse A nervousness that first-time homebuyers tend to feel after signing a sales contract or closing the purchase of a house.

Call Date The periodic or continuous right a lender has to call for payment of the total remaining balance prior to the date of maturity.

Call Option A clause in a loan agreement that allows a lender to demand repayment of the entire principal balance at any time.

Cap A limit on how much the monthly payment or interest rate is allowed to increase in an adjustable-rate mortgage.

Capital Appreciation The change in a property's or portfolio's market value after it has been adjusted for capital improvements and partial sales.

Capital Expenditures The purchase of long-term assets, or the expansion of existing ones, that prolongs the life or efficiency of those assets.

Capital Gain The amount of excess when the net proceeds from the sale of an asset are higher than its book value.

Capital Improvements Expenses that prolong the life of a property or add new improvements to it.

Capital Markets Public and private markets where individuals or businesses can raise or borrow capital.

Capitalization The mathematical process that investors use to derive the value of a property using the rate of return on investments.

Capitalization Rate The percentage of return as it is estimated from the net income of a property.

Carryback Financing A type of funding in which a seller agrees to hold back a note for a specified portion of the sales price.

Carrying Charges Costs incurred to the landlord when initially leasing out a property and then during the periods of vacancy.

Cash Flow The amount of income an investor receives on a rental property after operating expenses and loan payments have been deducted.

Cashier's Check A check the bank draws on its own resources instead of a depositor's account.

Cash-on-Cash Yield The percentage of a property's net cash flow and the average amount of invested capital during the specified operating year.

Cash-Out Refinance The act of refinancing a mortgage for an amount that is higher than the original amount for the purpose of using the leftover cash for personal use.

Certificate of Deposit A type of deposit that is held in a bank for a limited time and pays a certain amount of interest to the depositor.

Certificate of Deposit Index (CODI) A rate that is based on interest rates of six-month CDs and is often used to determine interest rates for some ARMs.

Certificate of Eligibility A type of document that the Department of Veterans Affairs issues to verify the eligibility of a veteran for a VA loan.

Certificate of Occupancy (CO) A written document issued by a local government or building agency that states that a home or other building is inhabitable after meeting all building codes.

Certificate of Reasonable Value (CRV) An appraisal presented by the Department of Veterans Affairs that shows the current market value of a property.

Certificate of Veteran Status A document veterans or reservists receive if they have served 90 days of continuous active duty (including training time).

Chain of Title The official record of all transfers of ownership over the history of a piece of property.

Chapter 11 The part of the federal bankruptcy code that deals with reorganizations of businesses.

Chapter 7 The part of the federal bankruptcy code that deals with liquidations of businesses.

Circulation Factor The interior space that is required for internal office circulation and is not included in the net square footage.

Class A A property rating that is usually assigned to those that will generate the maximum rent per square foot, due to superior quality and/or location.

Class B A good property that most potential tenants would find desirable but lacks certain attributes that would bring in the top dollar.

Class C A building that is physically acceptable but offers few amenities, thereby becoming cost-effective space for tenants who are seeking a particular image.

Clear Title A property title that is free of liens, defects, or other legal encumbrances.

Clear-Span Facility A type of building, usually a warehouse or parking garage, consisting of vertical columns on the outer edges of the structure and clear spaces between the columns.

Closed-End Fund A mixed fund with a planned range of investor capital and a limited life.

Closing The final act of procuring a loan and title in which documents are signed between the buyer and seller and/or their respective representation and all money concerned in the contract changes hands.

Closing Costs The expenses that are related to the sale of real estate including loan, title, and appraisal fees and are beyond the price of the property itself.

Closing Statement See: Settlement Statement.

Cloud on Title Certain conditions uncovered in a title search that present a negative impact to the title for the property.

Commercial Mortgage-Backed Securities (CMBS) A type of securities that is backed by loans on commercial real estate.

Collateralized Mortgage Obligation (CMO) Debt that is fully based on a pool of mortgages.

Co-Borrower Another individual who is jointly responsible for the loan and is on the title to the property.

Cost of Funds Index (COFI) An index used to determine changes in the interest rates for certain ARMs.

Co-Investment Program A separate account for an insurance company or investment partnership in which two or more pension funds may co-invest their capital in an individual property or a portfolio of properties.

Co-Investment The condition that occurs when two or more pension funds or groups of funds are sharing ownership of a real estate investment.

Collateral The property for which a borrower has obtained a loan, thereby assuming the risk of losing the property if the loan is not repaid according to the terms of the loan agreement.

Collection The effort on the part of a lender, due to a borrower defaulting on a loan, which involves mailing and recording certain documents in the event that the foreclosure procedure must be implemented.

Commercial Mortgage A loan used to purchase a piece of commercial property or building.

Commercial Mortgage Broker A broker specialized in commercial mortgage applications.

Commercial Mortgage Lender A lender specialized in funding commercial mortgage loans.

Commingled Fund A pooled fund that enables qualified employee benefit plans to mix their capital in order to achieve professional management, greater diversification, or investment positions in larger properties.

Commission A compensation to salespeople that is paid out of the total amount of the purchase transaction.

Commitment The agreement of a lender to make a loan with given terms for a specific period.

Commitment Fee The fee a lender charges for the guarantee of specified loan terms, to be honored at some point in the future.

Common Area Assessments Sometimes called Homeowners' Association Fees. Charges paid to the homeowners' association by the individual unit owners, in a condominium or planned unit development (PUD), that are usually used to maintain the property and common areas.

Common Area Maintenance The additional charges the tenant must pay in addition to the base rent to pay for the maintenance of common areas.

Common Areas The portions of a building, land, and amenities, owned or managed by a planned unit development (PUD) or condominium's homeowners' association, that are used by all of the unit owners who share in the common expense of operation and maintenance.

Common Law A set of unofficial laws that were originally based on English customs and used to some extent in several states.

Community Property Property that is acquired by a married couple during the course of their marriage and is considered in many states to be owned jointly, unless certain circumstances are in play.

Comparable Sales Also called Comps or Comparables. The recent selling prices of similar properties in the area that are used to help determine the market value of a property.

Compound Interest The amount of interest paid on the principal balance of a mortgage in addition to accrued interest.

Concessions Cash, or the equivalent, that the landlord pays or allows in the form of rental abatement, additional tenant finish allowance, moving expenses, or other costs expended in order to persuade a tenant to sign a lease.

Condemnation A government agency's act of taking private property, without the owner's consent, for public use through the power of eminent domain.

Conditional Commitment A lender's agreement to make a loan providing the borrower meets certain conditions.

Conditional Sale A contract to sell a property that states that the seller will retain the title until all contractual conditions have been fulfilled.

Condominium A type of ownership in which all of the unit owners own the property, common areas, and buildings jointly, and have sole ownership in the unit to which they hold the title.

Condominium Conversion Changing an existing rental property's ownership to the condominium form of ownership.

Condominium Hotel A condominium project that involves registration desks, short-term occupancy, food and telephone services, and daily cleaning services, and is generally operated as a commercial hotel even though the units are individually owned.

Conduit A strategic alliance between lenders and unaffiliated organizations that acts as a source of funding by regularly purchasing loans, usually with a goal of pooling and securitizing them.

Conforming Loan A type of mortgage that meets the conditions to be purchased by Fannie Mae or Freddie Mac.

Construction Documents The drawings and specifications an architect and/or engineer provides to describe construction requirements for a project.

Construction Loan A short-term loan to finance the cost of construction, usually dispensed in stages throughout the construction project.

Construction Management The process of ensuring that the stages of the construction project are completed in a timely and seamless manner.

Construction-to-Permanent Loan A construction loan that can be converted to a longer-term traditional mortgage after construction is complete.

Consultant Any individual or company that provides the services to institutional investors, such as defining real estate investment policies, making recommendations to advisers or managers, analyzing existing real estate portfolios, monitoring and reporting on portfolio performance, and/or reviewing specified investment opportunities.

Consumer Price Index (CPI) A measurement of inflation, relating to the change in the prices of goods and services that are regularly purchased by a specific population during a certain period of time.

Contiguous Space Refers to several suites or spaces on a floor (or connected floors) in a given building that can be combined and rented to a single tenant.

Contingency A specific condition that must be met before either party in a contract can be legally bound.

Contract An agreement, either verbal or written, to perform or not to perform a certain thing.

Contract Documents See: Construction Documents.

Contract Rent Also known as Face Rent. The dollar amount of the rental obligation specified in a lease.

Conventional Loan A long-term loan from a non-governmental lender that a borrower obtains for the purchase of a home.

Convertible Adjustable-Rate Mortgage A type of mortgage that begins as a traditional ARM but contains a provision to enable the borrower to change to a fixed-rate mortgage during a certain period of time.

Convertible Debt The point in a mortgage at which the lender has the option to convert to a partially or fully owned property within a certain period of time.

Convertible Preferred Stock Preferred stock that can be converted to common stock under certain conditions that have been specified by the issuer.

Conveyance The act of transferring a property title between parties by deed.

Cooperative Also called a Co-op. A type of ownership by multiple residents of a multi-unit housing complex in which they all own shares in the cooperative corporation that owns the property, thereby having the right to occupy a particular apartment or unit.

Cooperative Mortgage Any loan that is related to a cooperative residential project.

Core Properties The main types of property, specifically office, retail, industrial, and multi-family.

Co-Signer A second individual or party who also signs a promissory note or loan agreement, thereby taking responsibility for the debt in the event that the primary borrower cannot pay.

Cost-Approach Improvement Value The current expenses for constructing a copy or replacement for an existing structure, but subtracting an estimate of the accrued depreciation.

Cost-Approach Land Value The estimated value of the basic interest in the land, as if it were available for development to its highest and best use.

Cost-of-Sale Percentage An estimate of the expenses of selling an investment that represents brokerage commissions, closing costs, fees, and other necessary sales costs.

Coupon The token or expected interest rate the borrower is charged on a promissory note or mortgage.

Courier Fee The fee that is charged at closing for the delivery of documents between all parties concerned in a real estate transaction.

Covenant A written agreement, included in deeds or other legal documents, that defines the requirements for certain acts or use of a property.

Credit An agreement in which a borrower promises to repay the lender at a later date and receives something of value in exchange.

Credit Enhancement The necessary credit support, in addition to mortgage collateral, in order to achieve the desired credit rating on mortgage-backed securities.

Credit History An individual's record which details his current and past financial obligations and performance.

Credit Life Insurance A type of insurance that pays the balance of a mortgage if the borrower dies.

Credit Rating The degree of creditworthiness a person is assigned based on his credit history and current financial status.

Credit Report A record detailing an individual's credit, employment, and residence history used to determine the individual's creditworthiness.

Credit Repository A company that records and updates credit applicants' financial and credit information from various sources.

Credit Score Sometimes called a Credit Risk Score. The number contained in a consumer's credit report that represents a statistical summary of the information.

Creditor A party to whom other parties owe money.

Cross-Collateralization A group of mortgages or properties that jointly secures one debt obligation.

Cross-Defaulting A provision that allows a trustee or lender to require full payment on all loans in a group, if any single loan in the group is in default.

Cumulative Discount Rate A percentage of the current value of base rent with all landlord lease concessions taken into account.

Current Occupancy The current percentage of units in a building or property that is leased.

Current Yield The annual rate of return on an investment, expressed as a percentage.

Deal Structure The type of agreement in financing an acquisition. The deal can be un-leveraged, leveraged, traditional debt, participating debt, participating/convertible debt, or joint ventures.

Debt Any amount one party owes to another party.

Debt Service Coverage Ratio (DSCR) A property's yearly net operating income divided by the yearly cost of debt service.

Debt Service The amount of money that is necessary to meet all interest and principal payments during a specific period.

Debt-to-Income Ratio The percentage of a borrower's monthly payment on long-term debts divided by his gross monthly income.

Dedicate To change a private property to public ownership for a particular public use.

Deed A legal document that conveys property ownership to the buyer.

Deed in Lieu of Foreclosure A situation in which a deed is given to a lender in order to satisfy a mortgage debt and to avoid the foreclosure process.

Deed of Trust A provision that allows a lender to foreclose on a property in the event that the borrower defaults on the loan.

Default The state that occurs when a borrow fails to fulfill a duty or take care of an obligation, such as making monthly mortgage payments.

Deferred Maintenance Account A type of account that a borrower must fund to provide for maintenance of a property.

Deficiency Judgment The legal assignment of personal liability to a borrower for the unpaid balance of a mortgage, after foreclosing on the property has failed to yield the full amount of the debt.

Defined-Benefit Plan A type of benefit provided by an employer that defines an employee's benefits either as a fixed amount or a percentage of the beneficiary's salary when he retires.

Defined-Contribution Plan A type of benefit plan provided by an employer in which an employee's retirement benefits are determined by the amount that has been contributed by the employer and/or employee during the time of employment, and by the actual investment earnings on those contributions over the life of the fund.

Delinquency A state that occurs when the borrower fails to make mortgage payments on time, eventually resulting in foreclosure, if severe enough.

Delinquent Mortgage A mortgage in which the borrower is behind on payments.

Demising Wall The physical partition between the spaces of two tenants or from the building's common areas.

Deposit Also referred to as Earnest Money. The funds that the buyer provides when offering to purchase property.

Depreciation A decline in the value of property or an asset, often used as a tax-deductible item.

Derivative Securities A type of securities that has been created from other financial instruments.

Design/Build An approach in which a single individual or business is responsible for both the design and construction.

Disclosure A written statement, presented to a potential buyer, that lists information relevant to a piece of property, whether positive or negative.

Discount Points Fees that a lender charges in order to provide a lower interest rate.

Discount Rate A figure used to translate present value from future payments or receipts.

Discretion The amount of authority an adviser or manager is granted for investing and managing a client's capital.

Distraint The act of seizing a tenant's personal property when the tenant is in default, based on the right the landlord has in satisfying the debt.

Diversification The act of spreading individual investments out to insulate a portfolio against the risk of reduced yield or capital loss.

Dividend Yield The percentage of a security's market price that represents the annual dividend rate.

Dividend Distributions of cash or stock that stockholders receive.

Dividend-Ex Date The initial date on which a person purchasing the stock can no longer receive the most recently announced dividend.

Document Needs List The list of documents a lender requires from a potential borrower who is submitting a loan application.

Documentation Preparation Fee A fee that lenders, brokers, and/or settlement agents charge for the preparation of the necessary closing documents.

Dollar Stop An agreed amount of taxes and operating expenses each tenant must pay out on a prorated basis.

Down Payment The variance between the purchase price and the portion that the mortgage lender financed.

DOWNREIT A structure of organization that makes it possible for REITs to purchase properties using partnership units.

Draw A payment from the construction loan proceeds made to contractors, sub-contractors, home builders, or suppliers.

Due Diligence The activities of a prospective purchaser or mortgager of real property for the purpose of confirming that the property is as represented by the seller and is not subject to environmental or other problems.

Due on Sale Clause The standard mortgage language that states the loan must still be repaid if the property is resold.

Earnest Money See: Deposit.

Earthquake Insurance A type of insurance policy that provides coverage against earthquake damage to a home.

Easement The right given to a non-ownership party to use a certain part of the property for specified purposes, such as servicing power lines or cable lines.

Economic Feasibility The viability of a building or project in terms of costs and revenue where the degree of viability is established by extra revenue.

Economic Rent The market rental value of a property at a particular point in time.

Effective Age An estimate of the physical condition of a building presented by an appraiser.

Effective Date The date on which the sale of securities can commence once a registration statement becomes effective.

Effective Gross Income (EGI) The total property income that rents and other sources generate after subtracting a vacancy factor estimated to be appropriate for the property.

Effective Gross Rent (EGR) The net rent that is generated after adjusting for tenant improvements and other capital costs, lease commissions, and other sales expenses.

Effective Rent The actual rental rate that the landlord achieves after deducting the concession value from the base rental rate a tenant pays.

Electronic Authentication A way of providing proof that a particular electronic document is genuine, has arrived unaltered, and came from the indicated source.

Eminent Domain The power of the government to pay the fair market value for a property, appropriating it for public use.

Encroachment Any improvement or upgrade that illegally intrudes onto another party's property.

Encumbrance Any right or interest in a property that interferes with using it or transferring ownership.

End Loan The result of converting to permanent financing from a construction loan.

Entitlement A benefit of a VA home loan. Often referred to as Eligibility.

Environmental Impact Statement Legally required documents that must accompany major project proposals where there will likely be an impact on the surrounding environment.

Equal Credit Opportunity Act (ECOA) A federal law that requires a lender or other creditor to make credit available for applicants regardless of sex, marital status, race, religion, or age.

Equifax One of the three primary credit-reporting bureaus.

Equity The value of a property after existing liabilities have been deducted.

Employee Retirement Income Security Act (ERISA) A legislation that controls the investment activities, mainly of corporate and union pension plans.

Errors and Omissions Insurance A type of policy that insures against the mistakes of a builder or architect.

Escalation Clause The clause in a lease that provides for the rent to be increased to account for increases in the expenses the landlord must pay.

Escrow A valuable item, money, or documents deposited with a third party for delivery upon the fulfillment of a condition.

Escrow Account Also referred to as an Impound Account. An account established by a mortgage lender or servicing company for the purpose of holding funds for the payment of items, such as homeowner's insurance and property taxes.

Escrow Agent A neutral third party who makes sure that all conditions of a real estate transaction have been met before any funds are transferred or property is recorded.

Escrow Agreement A written agreement between an escrow agent and the contractual parties that defines the basic obligations of each party, the money (or other valuables) to be deposited in escrow, and how the escrow agent is to dispose of the money on deposit.

Escrow Analysis An annual investigation a lender performs to make sure they are collecting the appropriate amount of money for anticipated expenditures.

Escrow Closing The event in which all conditions of a real estate transaction have been met, and the property title is transferred to the buyer.

Escrow Company A neutral company that serves as a third party to ensure that all conditions of a real estate transaction are met.

Escrow Disbursements The dispensing of escrow funds for the payment of real estate taxes, hazard insurance, mortgage insurance, and other property expenses as they are due.

Escrow Payment The funds that are withdrawn by a mortgage servicer from a borrower's escrow account to pay property taxes and insurance.

Estate The total assets, including property, of an individual after he has died.

Estimated Closing Costs An estimation of the expenses relating to the sale of real estate.

Estimated Hazard Insurance An estimation of hazard insurance, or homeowner's insurance, that will cover physical risks.

Estimated Property Taxes An estimation of the property taxes that must be paid on the property, according to state and county tax rates.

Estoppel Certificate A signed statement that certifies that certain factual statements are correct as of the date of the statement and can be relied upon by a third party, such as a prospective lender or purchaser.

Eviction The legal removal of an occupant from a piece of property.

Examination of Title A title company's inspection and report of public records and other documents for the purpose of determining the chain of ownership of a property.

Exclusive Agency Listing A written agreement between a property owner and a real estate broker in which the owner promises to pay the broker a commission if certain property is leased during the listing period.

Exclusive Listing A contract that allows a licensed real estate agent to be the only agent who can sell a property for a given time.

Executed Contract An agreement in which all parties involved have fulfilled their duties.

Executor The individual who is named in a will to administer an estate. Executrix is the feminine form.

Exit Strategy An approach investors may use when they wish to liquidate all or part of their investment.

Experian One of the three primary credit-reporting bureaus.

Face Rental Rate The rental rate that the landlord publishes.

Facility Space The floor area in a hospitality property that is dedicated to activities, such as restaurants, health clubs, and gift shops, that interactively service multiple people and is not directly related to room occupancy.

Funds Available for Distribution (FAD) The income from operations, with cash expenditures subtracted, that may be used for leasing commissions and tenant improvement costs.

FAD Multiple The price per share of a REIT divided by its funds available for distribution.

Fair Credit Reporting Act (FCRA) The federal legislation that governs the processes credit reporting agencies must follow.

Fair Housing Act The federal legislation that prohibits the refusal to rent or sell to anyone based on race, color, religion, sex, family status, or disability.

Fair Market Value The highest price that a buyer would be willing to pay, and the lowest a seller would be willing to accept.

Fannie Mae See: Federal National Mortgage Association.

Fannie Mae's Community Home Buyer's Program A community lending model based on borrower income in which mortgage insurers and Fannie Mae offer flexible underwriting guidelines in order to increase the buying power for a low- or moderate-income family and to decrease the total amount of cash needed to purchase a home.

Farmer's Home Administration (FMHA) An agency within the U.S. Department of Agriculture that provides credit to farmers and other rural residents.

Federal Home Loan Mortgage Corporation (FHLMC) Also known as Freddie Mac. The company that buys mortgages from lending institutions, combines them with other loans, and sells shares to investors.

Federal Housing Administration (FHA) A government agency that provides low-rate mortgages to buyers who are able to make a down payment as low as 3 percent.

Federal National Mortgage Association (FNMA) Also known as Fannie Mae. A congressionally chartered, shareholder-owned company that is the nation's largest supplier of home mortgage funds. The company buys mortgages from lenders and resells them as securities on the secondary mortgage market.

Fee Simple The highest possible interest a person can have in a piece of real estate.

Fee Simple Estate An unconditional, unlimited inheritance estate in which the owner may dispose of or use the property as desired.

Fee Simple Interest The state of owning all the rights in a real estate parcel.

Funds From Operations (FFO) A ratio that is meant to highlight the amount of cash a company's real estate portfolio generates relative to its total operating cash flow.

FFO Multiple The price of a REIT share divided by its funds from operations.

FHA Loans Mortgages that the Federal Housing Administration (FHA) insures.

FHA Mortgage Insurance A type of insurance that requires a fee to be paid at closing in order to insure the loan with the Federal Housing Administration (FHA).

Fiduciary Any individual who holds authority over a plan's asset management, administration or disposition, or renders paid investment advice regarding a plan's assets.

Finance Charge The amount of interest to be paid on a loan or credit card balance.

Firm Commitment A written agreement a lender makes to loan money for the purchase of property.

First Mortgage The main mortgage on a property.

First Refusal Right/ Right of First Refusal A lease clause that gives a tenant the first opportunity to buy a property or to lease additional space in a property at the same price and terms as those contained in an offer from a third party that the owner has expressed a willingness to accept.

First-Generation Space A new space that has never before been occupied by a tenant and is currently available for lease.

First-Loss Position A security's position that will suffer the first economic loss if the assets below it lose value or are foreclosed on.

Fixed Costs Expenses that remain the same despite the level of sales or production.

Fixed Rate An interest rate that does not change over the life of the loan.

Fixed Time The particular weeks of a year that the owner of a timeshare arrangement can access his or her accommodations.

Fixed-Rate Mortgage A loan with an unchanging interest rate over the life of the loan.

Fixture Items that become a part of the property when they are permanently attached to the property.

Flat Fee An amount of money that an adviser or manager receives for managing a portfolio of real estate assets.

Flex Space A building that provides a flexible configuration of office or showroom space combined with manufacturing, laboratory, warehouse, distribution, etc.

Float The number of freely traded shares owned by the public.

Flood Certification The process of analyzing whether a property is located in a known flood zone.

Flood Insurance A policy that is required in designated flood zones to protect against loss due to flood damage.

Floor Area Ratio (FAR) A measurement of a building's gross square footage compared to the square footage of the land on which it is located.

For Sale By Owner (FSBO) A method of selling property in which the property owner serves as the selling agent and directly handles the sales process with the buyer or buyer's agent.

Force Majeure An external force that is not controlled by the contractual parties and prevents them from complying with the provisions of the contract.

Foreclosure The legal process in which a lender takes over ownership of a property once the borrower is in default in a mortgage arrangement.

Forward Commitments Contractual agreements to perform certain financing duties according to any stated conditions.

Four Quadrants of the Real Estate Capital Markets The four market types that consist of Private Equity, Public Equity, Private Debt, and Public Debt.

Freddie Mac See: Federal Home Loan Mortgage Corporation.

Front-End Ratio The measurement a lender uses to compare a borrower's monthly housing expense to gross monthly income.

Full Recourse A loan on which the responsibility of a loan is transferred to an endorser or guarantor in the event of default by the borrower.

Full-Service Rent A rental rate that includes all operating expenses and real estate taxes for the first year.

Fully Amortized ARM An ARM with a monthly payment that is sufficient to amortize the remaining balance at the current interest accrual rate over the amortization term.

Fully Diluted Shares The number of outstanding common stock shares if all convertible securities were converted to common shares.

Future Proposed Space The space in a commercial development that has been proposed but is not yet under construction, or the future phases of a multi-phase project that has not yet been built.

General Contractor The main person or business that contracts for the construction of an entire building or project, rather than individual duties.

General Partner The member in a partnership who holds the authority to bind the partnership and shares in its profits and losses.

Gift Money a buyer has received from a relative or other source that will not have to be repaid.

Ginnie Mae See: Government National Mortgage Association.

Going-In Capitalization Rate The rate that is computed by dividing the expected net operating income for the first year by the value of the property.

Good Faith Estimate A lender's or broker's estimate that shows all costs associated with obtaining a home loan including loan processing, title, and inspection fees.

Government Loan A mortgage that is insured or guaranteed by the FHA, the Department of Veterans Affairs (VA), or the Rural Housing Service (RHS).

Government National Mortgage Association (GNMA) Also known as Ginnie Mae. A government-owned corporation under the U.S. Department of Housing and Urban Development (HUD) that performs the same role as Fannie Mae and Freddie Mac in providing funds to lenders for making home loans, but only purchases loans that are backed by the federal government.

Grace Period A defined time period in which a borrower may make a loan payment after its due date without incurring a penalty.

Graduated Lease A lease, usually long-term, in which rent payments vary in accordance with future contingencies.

Graduated Payment Mortgage A mortgage that requires low payments during the first years of the loan, but eventually requires larger monthly payments over the term of the loan that become fixed later in the term.

Grant To give or transfer an interest in a property by deed or other documented method.

Grantee The party to whom an interest in a property is given.

Grantor The party who is transferring an interest in a property.

Gross Building Area The sum of areas at all floor levels, including the basement, mezzanine, and penthouses included in the principal outside faces of the exterior walls without allowing for architectural setbacks or projections.

Gross Income The total income of a household before taxes or expenses have been subtracted.

Gross Investment in Real Estate (Historic Cost) The total amount of equity and debt that is invested in a piece of real estate minus proceeds from sales or partial sales.

Gross Leasable Area The amount of floor space that is designed for tenants' occupancy and exclusive use.

Gross Lease A rental arrangement in which the tenant pays a flat sum for rent, and the landlord must pay all building expenses out of that amount.

Gross Real Estate Asset Value The total market value of the real estate investments under management in a fund or individual accounts, usually including the total value of all equity positions, debt positions, and joint venture ownership positions.

Gross Real Estate Investment Value The market value of real estate investments that are held in a portfolio without including debt.

Gross Returns The investment returns generated from operating a property without adjusting for adviser or manager fees.

Ground Lease Land being leased to an individual that has absolutely no residential dwelling on the property; or if it does, the ground (or land) is the only portion of the property being leased.

Ground Rent A long-term lease in which rent is paid to the land owner, normally to build something on that land.

Growing-Equity Mortgage A fixed-rate mortgage in which payments increase over a specified amount of time with the extra funds being applied to the principal.

Guarantor The part who makes a guaranty.

Guaranty An agreement in which the guarantor promises to satisfy the debt or obligations of another, if and when the debtor fails to do so.

Hard Cost The expenses attributed to actually constructing property improvements.

Hazard Insurance Also known as Homeowner's Insurance or Fire Insurance. A policy that provides coverage for damage from forces such as fire and wind.

Highest and Best Use The most reasonable, expected, legal use of a piece of vacant land or improved property that is physically possible, supported appropriately, financially feasible, and that results in the highest value.

High-Rise In a suburban district, any building taller than six stories. In a business district, any building taller than 25 stories.

Holdbacks A portion of a loan funding that is not dispersed until an additional condition is met, such as the completion of construction.

Holding Period The expected length of time, from purchase to sale, that an investor will own a property.

Hold-Over Tenant A tenant who retains possession of the leased premises after the lease has expired.

Home Equity Conversion Mortgage (HECM) Also referred to as a Reverse Annuity Mortgage. A type of mortgage in which the lender makes payments to the owner, thereby enabling older homeowners to convert equity in their homes into cash in the form of monthly payments.

Home Equity Line An open-ended amount of credit based on the equity a homeowner has accumulated.

Home Equity Loan A type of loan that allows owners to borrow against the equity in their homes up to a limited amount.

Home Inspection A pre-purchase examination of the condition a home is in by a certified inspector.

Home Inspector A certified professional who determines the structural soundness and operating systems of a property.

Home Price The price that a buyer and seller agree upon, generally based on the home's appraised market value.

Homeowners' Association (HOA) A group that governs a community, condominium building, or neighborhood and enforces the covenants, conditions, and restrictions set by the developer.

Homeowners' Association Dues The monthly payments that are paid to the homeowners' association for maintenance and communal expenses.

Homeowner's Insurance A policy that includes coverage for all damages that may affect the value of a house as defined in the terms of the insurance policy.

Homeowner's Warranty A type of policy homebuyers often purchase to cover repairs, such as heating or air-conditioning, should they stop working within the coverage period.

Homestead The property an owner uses as his primary residence.

Housing Expense Ratio The percentage of gross income that is devoted to housing costs each month.

HUD (Housing and Urban Development) A federal agency that oversees a variety of housing and community development programs, including the FHA.

HUD Median Income The average income for families in a particular area, which is estimated by HUD.

HUD-1 Settlement Statement Also known as the Closing Statement or Settlement Sheet. An itemized listing of the funds paid at closing.

HUD-1 Uniform Settlement Statement A closing statement for the buyer and seller that describes all closing costs for a real estate transaction or refinancing.

HVAC Heating, ventilating, and air-conditioning.

Hybrid Debt A position in a mortgage that has equity-like features of participation in both cash flow and the appreciation of the property at the point of sale or refinance.

Implied Cap Rate The net operating income divided by the sum of a REIT's equity market capitalization and its total outstanding debt.

Impounds The part of the monthly mortgage payment that is reserved in an account in order to pay for hazard insurance, property taxes, and private mortgage insurance.

Improvements The upgrades or changes made to a building to improve its value or usefulness.

Incentive Fee A structure in which the fee amount charged is based on the performance of the real estate assets under management.

Income Capitalization Value The figure derived for an income-producing property by converting its expected benefits into property value.

Income Property A particular property that is used to generate income but is not occupied by the owner.

Income Return The percentage of the total return generated by the income from property, fund, or account operations.

Index Financial table that lenders use for calculating interest rates on ARMs.

Indexed Rate The sum of the published index with a margin added.

Indirect Costs Expenses of development other than the costs of direct material and labor that are related directly to the construction of improvements.

Individual Account Management The process of maintaining accounts that have been established for individual plan sponsors or other investors for investment in real estate, where a firm acts as an adviser in obtaining and/or managing a real estate portfolio.

Inflation Hedge An investment whose value tends to increase at a greater rate than inflation, contributing to the preservation of the purchasing power of a portfolio.

Inflation The rate at which consumer prices increase each year.

Initial Interest Rate The original interest rate on an ARM which is sometimes subject to a variety of adjustments throughout the mortgage.

Initial Public Offering (IPO) The first time a previously private company offers securities for public sale.

Initial Rate Cap The limit specified by some ARMs as the maximum amount the interest rate may increase when the initial interest rate expires.

Initial Rate Duration The date specified by most ARMs at which the initial rate expires.

Inspection Fee The fee that a licensed property inspector charges for determining the current physical condition of the property.

Inspection Report A written report of the property's condition presented by a licensed inspection professional.

Institutional-Grade Property A variety of types of real estate properties usually owned or financed by tax-exempt institutional investors.

Insurance Binder A temporary insurance policy that is implemented while a permanent policy is drawn up or obtained.

Insurance Company Separate Account A real estate investment vehicle only offered by life insurance companies, which enables an ERISA-governed fund to avoid creating unrelated taxable income for certain types of property investments and investment structures.

Insured Mortgage A mortgage that is guaranteed by the FHA or by private mortgage insurance (PMI).

Interest Accrual Rate The rate at which a mortgage accrues interest.

Interest-Only Loan A mortgage for which the borrower pays only the interest that accrues on the loan balance each month.

Interest Paid over Life of Loan The total amount that has been paid to the lender during the time the money was borrowed.

Interest Rate The percentage that is charged for a loan.

Interest Rate Buy-Down Plans A plan in which a seller uses funds from the sale of the home to buy down the interest rate and reduce the buyer's monthly payments.

Interest Rate Cap The highest interest rate charge allowed on the monthly payment of an ARM during an adjustment period.

Interest Rate Ceiling The maximum interest rate a lender can charge for an ARM.

Interest Rate Floor The minimum possible interest rate a lender can charge for an ARM.

Interest The price that is paid for the use of capital.

Interest-Only Strip A derivative security that consists of all or part of the portion of interest in the underlying loan or security.

Interim Financing Also known as Bridge or Swing Loans. Short-term financing a seller uses to bridge the gap between the sale of one house and the purchase of another.

Internal Rate of Return (IRR) The calculation of a discounted cash flow analysis that is used to determine the potential total return of a real estate asset during a particular holding period.

Inventory The entire space of a certain proscribed market without concern for its availability or condition.

Investment Committee The governing body that is charged with overseeing corporate pension investments and developing investment policies for board approval.

Investment Manager An individual or company that assumes authority over a specified amount of real estate capital, invests that capital in assets using a separate account, and provides asset management.

Investment Policy A document that formalizes an institution's goals, objectives, and guidelines for asset management, investment advisory contracting, fees, and utilization of consultants and other outside professionals.

Investment Property A piece of real estate that generates some form of income.

Investment Strategy The methods used by a manager in structuring a portfolio and selecting the real estate assets for a fund or an account.

Investment Structures Approaches to investing that include un-leveraged acquisitions, leveraged acquisitions, traditional debt, participating debt, convertible debt, triple-net leases, and joint ventures.

Investment-Grade CMBS Commercial mortgage-backed securities that have ratings of AAA, AA, A, or BBB.

Investor Status The position an investor is in, either taxable or tax-exempt.

Joint Liability The condition in which responsibility rests with two or more people for fulfilling the terms of a home loan or other financial debt.

Joint Tenancy A form of ownership in which two or more people have equal shares in a piece of property, and rights pass to the surviving owner(s) in the event of death.

Joint Venture An investment business formed by more than one party for the purpose of acquiring or developing and managing property and/or other assets.

Judgment The decision a court of law makes.

Judicial Foreclosure The usual foreclosure proceeding some states use, which is handled in a civil lawsuit.

Jumbo Loan A type of mortgage that exceeds the required limits set by Fannie Mae and Freddie Mac each year.

Junior Mortgage A loan that is a lower priority behind the primary loan.

Just Compensation The amount that is fair to both the owner and the government when property is appropriated for public use through eminent domain.

Landlord's Warrant The warrant a landlord obtains to take a tenant's personal property to sell at a public sale to compel payment of the rent or other stipulation in the lease.

Late Charge Fee that is imposed by a lender when the borrower has not made a payment when it was due.

Late Payment Payment made to the lender after the due date has passed.

Lead Manager The investment banking firm that has primary responsibility for coordinating the new issuance of securities.

Lease A contract between a property owner and tenant that defines payments and conditions under which the tenant may occupy the real estate for a given period of time.

Lease Commencement Date The date at which the terms of the lease are implemented.

Lease Expiration Exposure Schedule A chart of the total square footage of all current leases that expire in each of the next five years, without taking renewal options into account.

Lease Option A financing option that provides for homebuyers to lease a home with an option to buy, with part of the rental payments being applied toward the down payment.

Leasehold Limited right to inhabit a piece of real estate held by a tenant.

Leasehold State A way of holding a property title in which the mortgagor does not actually own the property but has a long-term lease on it.

Leasehold Interest The right to hold or use property for a specific period of time at a given price without transferring ownership.

Lease-Purchase A contract that defines the closing date and solutions for the seller in the event that the buyer defaults.

Legal Blemish A negative count against a piece of property such as a zoning violation or fraudulent title claim.

Legal Description A way of describing and locating a piece of real estate that is recognized by law.

Legal Owner The party who holds the title to the property, although the title may carry no actual rights to the property other than as a lien.

Lender A bank or other financial institution that offers home loans.

Letter of Credit Promise from a bank or other party that the issuer will honor drafts or requests for payment upon complying with the requirements specified in the letter of credit.

Letter of Intent An initial agreement defining the proposed terms for the end contract.

Leverage Process of increasing the return on an investment by borrowing some of the funds at an interest rate less than the return on the project.

Liabilities Borrower's debts and financial obligations, whether long- or short-term.

Liability Insurance A type of policy that protects owners against negligence, personal injury, or property damage claims.

London InterBank Offered Rate (LIBOR) The interest rate offered on Euro-dollar deposits traded between banks and used to determine changes in interest rate for ARMs.

Lien A claim put by one party on the property of another as collateral for money owed.

Lien Waiver A waiver of a mechanic's lien rights that is sometimes required before the general contractor can receive money under the payment provisions of a construction loan and contract.

Life Cap A limit on the amount an ARM's interest rate can increase during the mortgage term.

Lifecycle The stages of development for a property: pre-development, development, leasing, operating, and rehabilitation.

Lifetime Payment Cap A limit on the amount that payments can increase or decrease over the life of an ARM.

Lifetime Rate Cap The highest possible interest rate that may be charged, under any circumstances, over the entire life of an ARM.

Like-Kind Property A term that refers to real estate that is held for productive use in a trade or business or for investment.

Limited Partnership A type of partnership in which some partners manage the business and are personally liable for partnership debts, but some partners contribute capital and share in profits without the responsibility of management.

Line of Credit An amount of credit granted by a financial institution up to a specified amount for a certain period of time to a borrower.

Liquid Asset A type of asset that can be easily converted into cash.

Liquidity The ease with which an individual's or company's assets can be converted to cash without losing their value.

Listing Agreement An agreement between a property owner and a real estate broker that authorizes the broker to attempt to sell or lease the property at a specified price and terms in return for a commission or other compensation.

Loan An amount of money that is borrowed and usually repaid with interest.

Loan Application A document that presents a borrower's income, debt, and other obligations to determine credit worthiness, as well as some basic information on the target property.

Loan Application Fee A fee lenders charge to cover expenses relating to reviewing a loan application.

Loan Commitment An agreement by a lender or other financial institution to make or ensure a loan for the specified amount and terms.

Loan Officer An official representative of a lending institution who is authorized to act on behalf of the lender within specified limits.

Loan Origination The process of obtaining and arranging new loans.

Loan Origination Fee A fee lenders charge to cover the costs related to arranging the loan.

Loan Servicing Process a lending institution goes through for all loans it manages. This involves processing payments, sending statements, managing the escrow/impound account, providing collection services on delinquent loans, ensuring that insurance and property taxes are made on the property, handling pay-offs and assumptions, as well as various other services.

Loan Term Time, usually expressed in years, that a lender sets in which a buyer must pay a mortgage.

Loan-to-Value (LTV) The ratio of the amount of the loan compared to the appraised value or sales price.

Lock-Box Structure An arrangement in which the payments are sent directly from the tenant or borrower to the trustee.

Lock-In A commitment from a lender to a borrower to guarantee a given interest rate for a limited amount of time.

Lock-In Period The period of time during which the borrower is guaranteed a specified interest rate.

Lockout The period of time during which a loan may not be paid off early.

Long-Term Lease A rental agreement that will last at least three years from initial signing to the date of expiration or renewal.

Loss Severity The percentage of lost principal when a loan is foreclosed.

Lot One of several contiguous parcels of a larger piece of land.

Low-Documentation Loan A mortgage that requires only a basic verification of income and assets.

Low-Rise A building that involves fewer than four stories above the ground level.

Lump-Sum Contract A type of construction contract that requires the general contractor to complete a building project for a fixed cost that is usually established beforehand by competitive bidding.

Magic Page A story of projected growth that describes how a new REIT will achieve its future plans for funds from operations or funds available for distribution.

Maintenance Fee The charge to homeowners' association members each month for the repair and maintenance of common areas.

Maker One who issues a promissory note and commits to paying the note when it is due.

Margin A percentage that is added to the index and fixed for the mortgage term.

Mark to Market The act of changing the original investment cost or value of a property or portfolio to the level of the current estimated market value.

Market Capitalization A measurement of a company's value that is calculated by multiplying the current share price by the current number of shares outstanding.

Market Rental Rates The rental income that a landlord could most likely ask for a property in the open market, indicated by the current rents for comparable spaces.

Market Study A forecast of the demand for a certain type of real estate project in the future that includes an estimate of the square footage that could be absorbed and the rents that could be charged.

Market Value The price a property would sell for at a particular point in time in a competitive market.

Marketable Title Title that is free of encumbrances and can be marketed immediately to a willing purchaser.

Master Lease The primary lease that controls other subsequent leases and may cover more property than all subsequent leases combined.

Master Servicer An entity that acts on behalf of a trustee for security holders' benefit in collecting funds from a borrower, advancing funds in the event of delinquencies and, in the event of default, taking a property through foreclosure.

Maturity Date The date at which the total principal balance of a loan is due.

Mechanic's Lien A claim created for securing payment priority for the price and value of work performed and materials furnished in constructing, repairing, or improving a building or other structure.

Meeting Space The space in hotels that is made available to the public to rent for meetings, conferences, or banquets.

Merged Credit Report A report that combines information from the three primary credit-reporting agencies including: Equifax, Experian, and TransUnion.

Metes and Bounds The surveyed boundary lines of a piece of land described by listing the compass directions (bounds) and distances (metes) of the boundaries.

Mezzanine Financing A financing position somewhere between equity and debt, meaning that there are higher-priority debts above and equity below.

Mid-Rise A building which shows 4 to 8 stories above ground level. In a business district, buildings up to 25 stories may also be included.

Mixed-Use Term referring to space within a building or project which can be used for more than one activity.

Modern Portfolio Theory (MPT) Approach of quantifying risk and return in an asset portfolio which emphasizes the portfolio rather than the individual assets and how the assets perform in relation to each other.

Modification An adjustment in the terms of a loan agreement.

Modified Annual Percentage Rate (APR) An index of the cost of a loan based on the standard APR but adjusted for the amount of time the borrower expects to hold the loan.

Monthly Association Dues A payment due each month to a homeowners' association for expenses relating to maintenance and community operations.

Mortgage An amount of money that is borrowed to purchase a property using that property as collateral.

Mortgage Acceleration Clause A provision enabling a lender to require that the rest of the loan balance is paid in a lump sum under certain circumstances.

Mortgage Banker A financial institution that provides home loans using its own resources, often selling them to investors such as insurance companies or Fannie Mae.

Mortgage Broker An individual who matches prospective borrowers with lenders that the broker is approved to deal with.

Mortgage Broker Business A company that matches prospective borrowers with lenders that the broker is approved to deal with.

Mortgage Constant A figure comparing an amortizing mortgage payment to the outstanding mortgage balance.

Mortgage Insurance (MI) A policy, required by lenders on some loans, that covers the lender against certain losses that are incurred as a result of a default on a home loan.

Mortgage Insurance Premium (MIP) The amount charged for mortgage insurance, either to a government agency or to a private MI company.

Mortgage Interest Deduction The tax write-off that the IRS allows most homeowners to deduct for annual interest payments made on real estate loans.

Mortgage Life and Disability Insurance A type of term life insurance borrowers often purchase to cover debt that is left when the borrower dies or becomes too disabled to make the mortgage payments.

Mortgagee The financial institution that lends money to the borrower.

Mortgagor The person who requests to borrow money to purchase a property.

Multi-Dwelling Units A set of properties that provide separate housing areas for more than one family but only require a single mortgage.

Multiple Listing Service A service that lists real estate offered for sale by a particular real estate agent that can be shown or sold by other real estate agents within a certain area.

National Association of Real Estate Investment Trusts (NAREIT) The national, non-profit trade organization that represents the real estate investment trust industry.

National Council of Real Estate Investment Fiduciaries (NCREIF) A group of real estate professionals who serve on committees; sponsor research articles, seminars and symposiums; and produce the NCREIF Property Index.

NCREIF Property Index (NPI) A quarterly and yearly report presenting income and appreciation components.

Negative Amortization An event that occurs when the deferred interest on an ARM is added, and the balance increases instead of decreases.

Net Asset Value (NAV) The total value of an asset or property minus leveraging or joint venture interests.

Net Asset Value Per Share The total value of a REIT's current assets divided by outstanding shares.

Net Assets The total value of assets minus total liabilities based on market value.

Net Cash Flow The total income generated by an investment property after expenses have been subtracted.

Net Investment in Real Estate Gross investment in properties minus the outstanding balance of debt.

Net Investment Income The income or loss of a portfolio or business minus all expenses, including portfolio and asset management fees, but before gains and losses on investments are considered.

Net Operating Income (NOI) The pre-tax figure of gross revenue minus operating expenses and an allowance for expected vacancy.

Net Present Value (NPV) The sum of the total current value of incremental future cash flows plus the current value of estimated sales proceeds.

Net Purchase Price The gross purchase price minus any associated financed debt.

Net Real Estate Investment Value The total market value of all real estate minus property-level debt.

Net Returns The returns paid to investors minus fees to advisers or managers.

Net Sales Proceeds The income from the sale of an asset, or part of an asset, minus brokerage commissions, closing costs, and market expenses.

Net Square Footage The total space required for a task or staff position.

Net Worth The worth of an individual or company figured on the basis of a difference between all assets and liabilities.

No-Cash-Out Refinance Sometimes referred to as a Rate and Term Refinance. A refinancing transaction that is intended only to cover the balance due on the current loan and any costs associated with obtaining the new mortgage.

No-Cost Loan A loan for which there are no costs associated with the loan that are charged by the lender, but with a slightly higher interest rate.

No-Documentation Loan A type of loan application that requires no income or asset verification, usually granted based on strong credit with a large down payment.

Nominal Yield The yield investors receive before it is adjusted for fees, inflation, or risk.

Non-Assumption Clause A provision in a loan agreement that prohibits transferring a mortgage to another borrower without approval from the lender.

Non-Compete Clause A provision in a lease agreement that specifies that the tenant's business is the only one that may operate in the property in question, thereby preventing a competitor moving in next door.

Non-Conforming Loan Any loan that is too large or does not meet certain qualifications to be purchased by Fannie Mae or Freddie Mac.

Non-Discretionary Funds The funds that are allocated to an investment manager who must have approval from the investor for each transaction.

Non-Investment-Grade CMBS Also referred to as High-Yield CMBS. **Commercial mortgage-backed securities that have ratings of BB or B.**

Non-Liquid Asset A type of asset that is not turned into cash very easily.

Non-Performing Loan A loan agreement that cannot meet its contractual principal and interest payments.

Non-Recourse Debt A loan that limits the lender's options to collect on the value of the real estate in the event of a default by the borrower.

Nonrecurring Closing Costs Fees that are only paid one time in a given transaction.

Note A legal document requiring a borrower to repay a mortgage at a specified interest rate over a certain period of time.

Note Rate The interest rate that is defined in a mortgage note.

Notice of Default A formal written notification a borrower receives once the borrower is in default stating that legal action may be taken.

Offer A term that describes a specified price or spread to sell whole loans or securities.

One-Year Adjustable-Rate Mortgage ARM for which the interest rate changes annually, generally based on movements of a published index and a specified margin.

Open Space A section of land or water that has been dedicated for public or private use or enjoyment.

Open-End Fund A type of commingled fund with an infinite life, always accepting new investor capital and making new investments in property.

Operating Cost Escalation A clause that is intended to adjust rents to account for external standards such as published indexes, negotiated wage levels, or building-related expenses.

Operating Expense The regular costs associated with operating and managing a property.

Opportunistic A phrase that generally describes a strategy of holding investments in under-performing and/or under-managed assets with the expectation of increases in cash flow and/or value.

Option A condition in which the buyer pays for the right to purchase a property within a certain period of time without the obligation to buy.

Option ARM Loan A type of mortgage in which the borrower has a variety of payment options each month.

Original Principal Balance The total principal owed on a mortgage before a borrower has made a payment.

Origination Fee A fee that most lenders charge for the purpose of covering the costs associated with arranging the loan.

Originator A company that underwrites loans for commercial and/or multi-family properties.

Out-Parcel The individual retail sites located within a shopping center.

Overallotment A practice in which the underwriters offer and sell a higher number of shares than they had planned to purchase from the issuer.

Owner Financing A transaction in which the property seller agrees to finance all or part of the amount of the purchase.

Parking Ratio A figure, generally expressed as square footage, that compares a building's total rentable square footage to its total number of parking spaces.

Partial Payment An amount paid that is not large enough to cover the normal monthly payment on a mortgage loan.

Partial Sales The act of selling a real estate interest that is smaller than the whole property.

Partial Taking The appropriating of a portion of an owner's property under the laws of Eminent Domain.

Participating Debt Financing allowing the lender to have participatory rights to equity through increased income and/or residual value over the balance of the loan or original value at the time the loan is funded.

Party in Interest Any party that may hold an interest, including employers, unions, and, sometimes, fiduciaries.

Pass-Through Certificate A document that allows the holder to receive payments of principal and interest from the underlying pool of mortgages.

Payment Cap The maximum amount a monthly payment may increase on an ARM.

Payment Change Date The date on which a new payment amount takes effect on an ARM or GPM, usually in the month directly after the adjustment date.

Payout Ratio The percentage of the primary earnings per share, excluding unusual items, that are paid to common stockholders as cash dividends during the next 12 months.

Pension Liability The full amount of capital that is required to finance vested pension fund benefits.

Percentage Rent The amount of rent that is adjusted based on the percentage of gross sales or revenues the tenant receives.

Per-Diem Interest The interest that is charged or accrued daily.

Performance Bond A bond that a contractor posts to guarantee full performance of a contract in which the proceeds will be used for completing the contract or compensating the owner for loss in the event of nonperformance.

Performance Measurement The process of measuring how well an investor's real estate has performed regarding individual assets, advisers/managers, and portfolios.

Performance The changes each quarter in fund or account values that can be explained by investment income, realized or unrealized appreciation, and the total return to the investors before and after investment management fees.

Performance-Based Fees The fees that advisers or managers receive that are based on returns to investors.

Periodic Payment Cap The highest amount that payments can increase or decrease during a given adjustment period on an ARM.

Periodic Rate Cap The maximum amount that the interest rate can increase or decrease during a given adjustment period on an ARM.

Permanent Loan A long-term property mortgage.

Personal Property Any items belonging to a person that is not real estate.

PITI Principal, Interest, Taxes, Insurance. The items that are included in the monthly payment to the lender for an impounded loan, as well as mortgage insurance.

PITI Reserves The amount in cash that a borrower must readily have after the down payment and all closing costs are paid when purchasing a home.

Plan Assets The assets included in a pension plan.

Plan Sponsor The party that is responsible for administering an employee benefit plan.

Planned Unit Development (PUD) A type of ownership where individuals actually own the building or unit they live in, but common areas are owned jointly with the other members of the development or association. Contrast with condominium, where an individual actually owns the airspace of his unit, but the buildings and common areas are owned jointly with the others in the development or association.

Plat A chart or map of a certain area showing the boundaries of individual lots, streets, and easements.

Pledged Account Mortgage (PAM) A loan tied to a pledged savings account for which the fund and earned interest are used to gradually reduce mortgage payments.

Point Also referred to as a Discount Point. A fee a lender charges to provide a lower interest rate, equal to 1 percent of the amount of the loan.

Portfolio Management A process that involves formulating, modifying, and implementing a real estate investment strategy according to an investor's investment objectives.

Portfolio Turnover The amount of time averaged from the time an investment is funded until it is repaid or sold.

Power of Attorney A legal document that gives someone the authority to act on behalf of another party.

Power of Sale The clause included in a mortgage or deed of trust that provides the mortgagee (or trustee) with the right and power to advertise and sell the property at public auction if the borrower is in default.

Pre-Approval The complete analysis a lender makes regarding a potential borrower's ability to pay for a home as well as a confirmation of the proposed amount to be borrowed.

Pre-Approval Letter The letter a lender presents that states the amount of money they are willing to lend a potential buyer.

Preferred Shares Certain stocks that have a prior distributions claim up to a defined amount before the common shareholders may receive anything.

Pre-Leased A certain amount of space in a proposed building that must be leased before construction may begin or a certificate of occupancy may be issued.

Prepaid Expenses The amount of money that is paid before it is due, including taxes, insurance, and/or assessments.

Prepaid Fees The charges that a borrower must pay in advance regarding certain recurring items, such as interest, property taxes, hazard insurance, and PMI, if applicable.

Prepaid Interest The amount of interest that is paid before its due date.

Prepayment The money that is paid to reduce the principal balance of a loan before the date it is due.

Prepayment Penalty A penalty that may be charged to the borrower when he pays off a loan before the planned maturity date.

Prepayment Rights The right a borrower is given to pay the total principal balance before the maturity date free of penalty.

Prequalification The initial assessment by a lender of a potential borrower's ability to pay for a home as well as an estimate of how much the lender is willing to supply to the buyer.

Price-to-Earnings Ratio The comparison that is derived by dividing the current share price by the sum of the primary earnings per share from continuing operations over the past year.

Primary Issuance The preliminary financing of an issuer.

Prime Rate The best interest rate reserved for a bank's preferred customers.

Prime Space The first-generation space that is available for lease.

Prime Tenant The largest or highest-earning tenant in a building or shopping center.

Principal The amount of money originally borrowed in a mortgage, before interest is included and with any payments subtracted.

Principal Balance The total current balance of mortgage principal not including interest.

Principal Paid over Life of Loan The final total of scheduled payments to the principal that the lender calculates to equal the face amount of the loan.

Principal Payments The lender's return of invested capital.

Principle of Conformity The concept that a property will probably increase in value if its size, age, condition, and style are similar to other properties in the immediate area.

Private Debt Mortgages or other liabilities for which an individual is responsible.

Private Equity A real estate investment that has been acquired by a noncommercial entity.

Private Mortgage Insurance (PMI) A type of policy that a lender requires when the borrower's down payment or home equity percentage is under 20 percent of the value of the property.

Private Placement The sale of a security in a way that renders it exempt from the registration rules and requirements of the SEC.

Private REIT A real estate investment company that is structured as a real estate investment trust that places and holds shares privately rather than publicly.

Pro Rata The proportionate amount of expenses per tenant for the property's maintenance and operation.

Processing Fee A fee some lenders charge for gathering the information necessary to process the loan.

Production Acres The portion of land that can be used directly in agriculture or timber activities to generate income, but not areas used for such things as machinery storage or support.

Prohibited Transaction Certain transactions that may not be performed between a pension plan and a party in interest, such as the following: the sale, exchange or lease of any property; a loan or other grant of credit; and furnishing goods or services.

Promissory Note A written agreement to repay the specific amount over a certain period of time.

Property Tax The tax that must be paid on private property.

Prudent Man Rule The standard to which ERISA holds a fiduciary accountable.

Public Auction An announced public meeting held at a specified location for the purpose of selling property to repay a mortgage in default.

Public Debt Mortgages or other liabilities for which a commercial entity is responsible.

Public Equity A real estate investment that has been acquired by REITs and other publicly traded real estate operating companies.

Punch List An itemized list that documents incomplete or unsatisfactory items after the contractor has declared the space to be mostly complete.

Purchase Agreement The written contract the buyer and seller both sign defining the terms and conditions under which a property is sold.

Purchase Money Transaction A transaction in which property is acquired through the exchange of money or something of equivalent value.

Purchase-Money Mortgage (PMM) A mortgage obtained by a borrower that serves as partial payment for a property.

Qualified Plan Any employee benefit plan that the IRS has approved as a tax-exempt plan.

Qualifying Ratio The measurement a lender uses to determine how much they are willing to lend to a potential buyer.

Quitclaim Deed A written document that releases a party from any interest they may have in a property.

Rate Cap The highest interest rate allowed on a monthly payment during an adjustment period of an ARM.

Rate Lock The commitment of a lender to a borrower that guarantees a certain interest rate for a specific amount of time.

Rate-Improvement Mortgage A loan that includes a clause that entitles a borrower to a one-time-only cut in the interest rate without having to refinance.

Rating Agencies Independent firms that are engaged to rate securities' creditworthiness on behalf of investors.

Rating A figure that represents the credit quality or creditworthiness of securities.

Raw Land A piece of property that has not been developed and remains in its natural state.

Raw Space Shell space in a building that has not yet been developed.

Real Estate Agent An individual who is licensed to negotiate and transact the real estate sales.

Real Estate Fundamentals The factors that drive the value of property.

Real Estate Settlement Procedures Act (RESPA) A legislation for consumer protection that requires lenders to notify borrowers regarding closing costs in advance.

Real Property Land and anything else of a permanent nature that is affixed to the land.

Real Rate of Return The yield given to investors minus an inflationary factor.

Realtor A real estate agent or broker who is an active member of a local real estate board affiliated with the National Association of Realtors.

Recapture The act of the IRS recovering the tax benefit of a deduction or a credit that a taxpayer has previously taken in error.

Recorder A public official who records transactions that affect real estate in the area.

Recording The documentation that the registrar's office keeps of the details of properly executed legal documents.

Recording Fee A fee real estate agents charge for moving the sale of a piece of property into the public record.

Recourse Option a lender has for recovering losses against the personal assets of a secondary party who is also liable for a debt in default.

Red Herring An early prospectus that is distributed to prospective investors that includes a note in red ink on the cover stating that the SEC-approved registration statement is not yet in effect.

Refinance Transaction The act of paying off an existing loan using the funding gained from a new loan that uses the same property as security.

Regional Diversification Boundaries that are defined based on geography or economic lines.

Registration Statement The set of forms that are filed with the SEC (or the appropriate state agency) regarding a proposed offering of new securities or the listing of outstanding securities on a national exchange.

Regulation Z A federal legislation under the Truth in Lending Act that requires lenders to advise the borrower in writing of all costs that are associated with the credit portion of a financial transaction.

Rehab Short for Rehabilitation. Refers to an extensive renovation intended to extend the life of a building or project.

Rehabilitation Mortgage A loan meant to fund the repairing and improving of a resale home or building.

Real Estate Investment Trust (REIT) A trust corporation that combines the capital of several investors for the purpose of acquiring or providing funding for real estate.

Remaining Balance The amount of the principal on a home loan that has not yet been paid.

Remaining Term The original term of the loan after the number of payments made has been subtracted.

Real Estate Mortgage Investment Conduit (REMIC) An investment vehicle that is designed to hold a pool of mortgages solely to issue multiple classes of mortgage-backed securities in a way that avoids doubled corporate tax.

Renewal Option A clause in a lease agreement that allows a tenant to extend the term of a lease.

Renewal Probability The average percentage of a building's tenants who are expected to renew terms at market rental rates upon the lease expiration.

Rent Commencement Date The date at which a tenant is to begin paying rent.

Rent Loss Insurance A policy that covers loss of rent or rental value for a landlord due to any condition that renders the leased premises inhabitable, thereby excusing the tenant from paying rent.

Rent The fee paid for the occupancy and/or use of any rental property or equipment.

Rentable/Usable Ratio A total rentable area in a building divided by the area available for use.

Rental Concession See: Concessions.

Rental Growth Rate The projected trend of market rental rates over a particular period of analysis.

Rent-Up Period The period of time following completion of a new building when tenants are actively being sought and the project is stabilizing.

Real Estate Owned (REO) The real estate that a savings institution owns as a result of foreclosure on borrowers in default.

Repayment Plan An agreement made to repay late installments or advances.

Replacement Cost Projected cost by current standards of constructing a building that is equivalent to the building being appraised.

Replacement Reserve Fund Money that is set aside for replacing of common property in a condominium, PUD, or cooperative project.

Request for Proposal (RFP) A formal request that invites investment managers to submit information regarding investment strategies, historical investment performance, current investment opportunities, investment management fees, and other pension fund client relationships used by their firm.

Rescission The legal withdrawing of a contract or consent from the parties involved.

Reserve Account An account that must be funded by the borrower to protect the lender.

Resolution Trust Corp. (RTC) The congressional corporation established for the purpose of containing, managing, and selling failed financial institutions, thereby recovering taxpayer funds.

Retail Investor An investor who sells interests directly to consumers.

Retention Rate The percentage of trailing year's earnings that have been dispersed into the company again. It is calculated as 100 minus the trailing 12-month payout ratio.

Return on Assets The measurement of the ability to produce net profits efficiently by making use of assets.

Return on Equity The measurement of the return on the investment in a business or property.

Return on Investments The percentage of money that has been gained as a result of certain investments.

Reverse Mortgage See: Home Equity Conversion Mortgage.

Reversion Capitalization Rate The capitalization rate that is used to derive reversion value.

Reversion Value A benefit that an investor expects to receive as a lump sum at the end of an investment.

Revolving Debt A credit arrangement that enables a customer to borrow against a predetermined line of credit when purchasing goods and services.

Revenue per Available Room (RevPAR) The total room revenue for a particular period divided by the average number of rooms available in a hospitality facility.

Right of Ingress or Egress The option to enter or to leave the premises in question.

Right of Survivorship The option that survivors have to take on the interest of a deceased joint tenant.

Right to Rescission A legal provision that enables borrowers to cancel certain loan types within three days after they sign.

Risk Management A logical approach to analyzing and defining insurable and non-insurable risks while evaluating the availability and costs of purchasing third-party insurance.

Risk-Adjusted Rate of Return A percentage that is used to identify investment options that are expected to deliver a positive premium despite their volatility.

Road Show A tour of the executives of a company that is planning to go public, during which the executives travel to a variety of cities to make presentations to underwriters and analysts regarding their company and IPO.

Roll-Over Risk The possibility that tenants will not renew their lease.

Sale-Leaseback An arrangement in which a seller deeds a property, or part of it, to a buyer in exchange for money or the equivalent, then leases the property from the new owner.

Sales Comparison Value A value that is calculated by comparing the appraised property to similar properties in the area that have been recently sold.

Sales Contract An agreement that both the buyer and seller sign defining the terms of a property sale.

Second Mortgage A secondary loan obtained on a piece of property.

Secondary Market A market in which existing mortgages are bought and sold as part of a mortgages pool.

Secondary (Follow-On) Offering An offering of stock made by a company that is already public.

Second-Generation or Secondary Space Space that has been occupied before and becomes available for lease again, either by the landlord or as a sublease.

Secured Loan A loan that is secured by some sort of collateral.

Securities and Exchange Commission (SEC) The federal agency that oversees the issuing and exchanging of public securities.

Securitization The act of converting a non-liquid asset into a tradable form.

Security The property or other asset that will serve as a loan's collateral.

Security Deposit An amount of money a tenant gives to a landlord to secure the performance of terms in a lease agreement.

Seisen (Seizen) The ownership of real property under a claim of freehold estate.

Self-Administered REIT A REIT in which the management are employees of the REIT or similar entity.

Self-Managed REIT See: Self-Administered REIT.

Seller Carry-Back An arrangement in which the seller provides the financing to purchase a home.

Seller Financing A type of funding in which the borrower may use part of the equity in the property to finance the purchase.

Senior Classes The security classes who have the highest priority for receiving payments from the underlying mortgage loans.

Separate Account A relationship in which a single pension plan sponsor is used to retain an investment manager or adviser under a stated investment policy exclusively for that sponsor.

Servicer An organization that collects principal and interest payments from borrowers and manages borrowers' escrow accounts on behalf of a trustee.

Servicing The process of collecting mortgage payments from borrowers as well as related responsibilities.

Setback The distance required from a given reference point before a structure can be built.

Settlement or Closing Fees The fees that the escrow agent receives for carrying out the written instructions in the agreement between borrower and lender and/or buyer and seller.

Settlement Statement See: HUD-1 Settlement Statement.

Shared-Appreciation Mortgage A loan that enables a lender or other party to share in the profits of the borrower when the borrower sells the home.

Shared-Equity Transaction A transaction in which two people purchase a property, one as a residence and the other as an investment.

Shares Outstanding The number of shares of outstanding common stock minus the treasury shares.

Site Analysis A determination of how suitable a specific parcel of land is for a particular use.

Site Development The implementation of all improvements that are needed for a site before construction may begin.

Site Plan A detailed description and map of the location of improvements to a parcel.

Slab The flat, exposed surface that is laid over the structural support beams to form the building's floor(s).

Social Investing A strategy in which investments are driven in partially or completely by social or non-real estate objectives.

Soft Cost The part of an equity investment, aside from the literal cost of the improvements, that could be tax-deductible in the first year.

Space Plan A chart or map of space requirements for a tenant that includes wall/door locations, room sizes, and even furniture layouts.

Special Assessment Certain charges that are levied against real estates for public improvements to benefit the property in question.

Special Servicer A company that is hired to collect on mortgages that are either delinquent or in default.

Specified Investing A strategy of investment in individually specified properties, portfolios, or commingled funds are fully or partially detailed prior to the commitment of investor capital.

Speculative Space Any space in a rental property that has not been leased prior to construction on a new building begins.

Stabilized Net Operating Income Expected income minus expenses that reflect relatively stable operations.

Stabilized Occupancy The best projected range of long-term occupancy that a piece of rental property will achieve after existing in the open market for a reasonable period of time with terms and conditions that are comparable to similar offerings.

Step-Rate Mortgage A loan that allows for a gradual interest rate increase during the first few years of the loan.

Step-Up Lease (Graded Lease) A lease agreement that specifies certain increases in rent at certain intervals during the complete term of the lease.

Straight Lease (Flat Lease) A lease agreement that specifies an amount of rent that should be paid regularly during the complete term of the lease.

Strip Center Any shopping area that is made up of a row of stores but is not large enough to be anchored by a grocery store.

Subcontractor A contractor who has been hired by the general contractor, often specializing in a certain required task for the construction project.

Subdivision The most common type of housing development created by dividing a larger tract of land into individual lots for sale or lease.

Sublessee A person or business that holds the rights of use and occupancy under a lease contract with the original lessee, who still retains primary responsibility for the lease obligations.

Subordinate Financing Any loan with a priority lower than loans that were obtained beforehand.

Subordinate Loan A second or third mortgage obtained with the same property being used as collateral.

Subordinated Classes Classes that have the lowest priority of receiving payments from underlying mortgage loans.

Subordination The act of sharing credit loss risk at varying rates among two or more classes of securities.

Subsequent Rate Adjustments The interest rate for ARMs that adjusts at regular intervals, sometimes differing from the duration period of the initial interest rate.

Subsequent Rate Cap Maximum amount the interest rate may increase at each regularly scheduled interest rate adjustment date on an ARM.

Super Jumbo Mortgage A loan that is over $650,000 for some lenders or $1,000,000 for others.

Surety A person who willingly binds himself to the debt or obligation of another party.

Surface Rights A right or easement that is usually granted with mineral rights that enables the holder to drill through the surface.

Survey A document or analysis containing the precise measurements of a piece of property as performed by a licensed surveyor.

Sweat Equity The non-cash improvements in value that an owner adds to a piece of property.

Synthetic Lease A transaction that is considered to be a lease by accounting standards but a loan by tax standards.

Taking Similar to condemning, or any other interference with rights to private property, but a physical seizure or appropriation is not required.

Tax Base The determined value of all property that lies within the jurisdiction of the taxing authority.

Tax Lien A type of lien placed against a property if the owner has not paid property or personal taxes.

Tax Roll Record that contains the descriptions of all land parcels and their owners that is located within the county.

Tax Service Fee A fee that is charged for the purpose of setting up monitoring of the borrower's property tax payments by a third party.

Teaser Rate A small, short-term interest rate offered on a mortgage in order to convince the potential borrower to apply.

Tenancy by the Entirety A form of ownership held by spouses in which they both hold title to the entire property with right of survivorship.

Tenancy in Common A type of ownership held by two or more owners in an undivided interest in the property with no right of survivorship.

Tenant (Lessee) A party who rents a piece of real estate from another by way of a lease agreement.

Tenant at Will A person who possesses a piece of real estate with the owner's permission.

Tenant Improvement (TI) Allowance The specified amount of money that the landlord contributes toward tenant improvements.

Tenant Improvement (TI) The upgrades or repairs that are made to the leased premises by or for a tenant.

Tenant Mix The quality of the income stream for a property.

Term The length that a loan lasts or is expected to last before it is repaid.

Third-Party Origination A process in which another party is used by the lender to originate, process, underwrite, close, fund, or package the mortgages it expects to deliver to the secondary mortgage market.

Timeshare A form of ownership involving purchasing a specific period of time or percentage of interest in a vacation property.

Time-Weighted Average Annual Rate of Return The regular yearly return over several years that would have the same return value as combining the actual annual returns for each year in the series.

Title The legal written document that provides someone ownership in a piece of real estate.

Title Company A business that determines that a property title is clear and that provides title insurance.

Title Exam An analysis of the public records in order to confirm that the seller is the legal owner, and there are no encumbrances on the property.

Title Insurance A type of policy that is issued to both lenders and buyers to cover loss due to property ownership disputes that may arise at a later date.

Title Insurance Binder A written promise from the title insurance company to insure the title to the property, based on the conditions and exclusions shown in the binder.

Title Risk The potential impediments in transferring a title from one party to another.

Title Search The process of analyzing all transactions existing in the public record in order to determine whether any title defects could interfere with the clear transfer of property ownership.

Total Acres The complete amount of land area that is contained within a real estate investment.

Total Assets The final amount of all gross investments, cash and equivalents, receivables, and other assets as they are presented on the balance sheet.

Total Commitment The complete funding amount that is promised once all specified conditions have been met.

Total Expense Ratio The comparison of monthly debt obligations to gross monthly income.

Total Inventory The total amount of square footage commanded by property within a geographical area.

Total Lender Fees Charges that the lender requires for obtaining the loan, aside from other fees associated with the transfer of a property.

Total Loan Amount The basic amount of the loan plus any additional financed closing costs.

Total Monthly Housing Costs The amount that must be paid each month to cover principal, interest, property taxes, PMI, and/or either hazard insurance or homeowners' association dues.

Total of All Payments The total cost of the loan after figuring the sum of all monthly interest payments.

Total Principal Balance The sum of all debt, including the original loan amount adjusted for subsequent payments and any unpaid items that may be included in the principal balance by the mortgage note or by law.

Total Retail Area The total floor area of a retail center that is currently leased or available for lease.

Total Return The final amount of income and appreciation returns per quarter.

Townhouse An attached home that is not considered to be a condominium.

Trade Fixtures Any personal property that is attached to a structure and used in the business but is removable once the lease is terminated.

Trading Down The act of purchasing a property that is less expensive than the one currently owned.

Trading Up The act of purchasing a property that is more expensive than the one currently owned.

Tranche A class of securities that may or may not be rated.

TransUnion Corporation One of the primary credit-reporting bureaus.

Transfer of Ownership Any process in which a property changes hands from one owner to another.

Transfer Tax An amount specified by state or local authorities when ownership in a piece of property changes hands.

Treasury Index A measurement that is used to derive interest rate changes for ARMs.

Triple Net Lease A lease that requires the tenant to pay all property expenses on top of the rental payments.

Trustee A fiduciary who oversees property or funds on behalf of another party.

Truth-in-Lending The federal legislation requiring lenders to fully disclose the terms and conditions of a mortgage in writing.

TurnKey Project A project in which all components are within a single supplier's responsibility.

Two- to Four-Family Property A structure that provides living space for two to four families while ownership is held in a single deed.

Two-Step Mortgage An ARM with two different interest rates: one for the loan's first five or seven years and another for the remainder of the loan term.

Under Construction The time period that exists after a building's construction has started but before a certificate of occupancy has been presented.

Under Contract The period of time during which a buyer's offer to purchase a property has been accepted, and the buyer is able to finalize financing arrangements without the concern of the seller making a deal with another buyer.

Underwriter A company, usually an investment banking firm, that is involved in a guarantee that an entire issue of stocks or bonds will be purchased.

Underwriters' Knot An approved knot according to code that may be tied at the end of an electrical cord to prevent the wires from being pulled away from their connection to each other or to electrical terminals.

Underwriting The process during which lenders analyze the risks a particular borrower presents and set appropriate conditions for the loan.

Underwriting Fee A fee that mortgage lenders charge for verifying the information on the loan application and making a final decision on approving the loan.

Unencumbered A term that refers to property free of liens or other encumbrances.

Unimproved Land See: Raw Land.

Unrated Classes Usually the lowest classes of securities.

Unrecorded Deed A deed that transfers right of ownership from one owner to another without being officially documented.

Umbrella Partnership Real Estate Investment Trust (UPREIT) An organizational structure in which a REIT's assets are owned by a holding company for tax reasons.

Usable Square Footage The total area that is included within the exterior walls of the tenant's space.

Use The particular purpose for which a property is intended to be employed.

VA Loan A mortgage through the VA program in which a down payment is not necessarily required.

Vacancy Factor The percentage of gross revenue that pro-forma income statements expect to be lost due to vacancies.

Vacancy Rate The percentage of space that is available to rent.

Vacant Space Existing rental space that is presently being marketed for lease minus space that is available for sublease.

Value-Added A phrase advisers and managers generally use to describe investments in underperforming and/or under-managed assets.

Variable Rate Mortgage (VRM) A loan in which the interest rate changes according to fluctuations in particular indexes.

Variable Rate Also called adjustable rate. The interest rate on a loan that varies over the term of the loan according to a predetermined index.

Variance A permission that enables a property owner to work around a zoning ordinance's literal requirements which cause a unique hardship due to special circumstances.

Verification of Deposit (VOD) The confirmation statement a borrower's bank may be asked to sign in order to verify the borrower's account balances and history.

Verification of Employment (VOE) The confirmation statement a borrower's employer may be asked to sign in order to verify the borrower's position and salary.

Vested Having the right to draw on a portion or on all of a pension or other retirement fund.

Veterans Affairs (VA) A federal government agency that assists veterans in purchasing a home without a down payment.

Virtual Storefront A retail business presence on the Internet.

Waiting Period The period of time between initially filing a registration statement and the date it becomes effective.

Warehouse Fee A closing cost fee that represents the lender's expense of temporarily holding a borrower's loan before it is sold on the secondary mortgage market.

Weighted-Average Coupon The average, using the balance of each mortgage as the weighting factor, of the gross interest rates of the mortgages underlying a pool as of the date of issue.

Weighted-Average Equity The part of the equation that is used to calculate investment-level income, appreciation, and total returns on a quarter-by-quarter basis.

Weighted-Average Rental Rates The average ratio of unequal rental rates across two or more buildings in a market.

Working Drawings The detailed blueprints for a construction project that comprise the contractual documents which describe the exact manner in which a project is to be built.

Workout The strategy in which a borrower negotiates with a lender to attempt to restructure the borrower's debt rather than go through the foreclosure proceedings.

Wraparound Mortgage A loan obtained by a buyer to use for the remaining balance on the seller's first mortgage, as well as an additional amount requested by the seller.

Write-Down A procedure used in accounting when an asset's book value is adjusted downward to reflect current market value more accurately.

Write-Off A procedure used in accounting when an asset is determined to be uncollectible and is therefore considered to be a loss.

Yield Maintenance Premium A penalty the borrower must pay in order to make investors whole in the event of early repayment of principal.

Yield Spread The difference in income derived from a commercial mortgage and from a benchmark value.

Yield The actual return on an investment, usually paid in dividends or interest.

Zoning Ordinance The regulations and laws that control the use or improvement of land in a particular area or zone.

Zoning The act of dividing a city or town into particular areas and applying laws and regulations regarding the architectural design, structure, and intended uses of buildings within those areas.

Index

Author Biography

Dan Blacharski has been a professional writer and online entrepreneur for over 25 years. He has written six books and has ghostwritten several others; has produced thousands of print and online features, articles, and columns; and has helped many internet companies jump into the fray. A refugee from Silicon Valley, Dan was there during the "dot-com boom," witnessing firsthand the incredible rise and fall of countless empires, and gaining insight into what makes a new-era internet company succeed or fail. He worked directly with many of these companies, helping them to refine their messaging. As far as real estate, Dan prefers no-money-down deals and spends time renovating his own fixer-upper, a 120-year old restored Victorian in the historic district of South Bend, Indiana.

Dan currently lives in South Bend with his lovely wife Charoenkwan; but having never gotten quite used to the frigid Midwest, they spend their winters in Bangkok.